India and the Changing Geopolitics of Oil

The global energy scenario has transformed in the past 20 years. Oil demand, earlier driven by the West, is now shifting to the East, more specifically to Asia. New oil supplies from North America have challenged the hegemony of the traditional oil exporters from West Asia and Africa. India, once a marginal player in the world oil market, is now a valued customer providing demand security to oil exporters.

This book systematically examines India's oil and gas trade, which makes it the world's third largest importer of oil after China and the US. It explores the changing patterns of oil demand and supply, and the growing market for natural gas, renewable energy, biofuel, and alternative sources of energy. Further, the volume discusses a range of issues that affects India's position in the global energy economy, such as

- The geographic shifts in energy production and trade; international relations and economic sanctions that affect the oil trade;
- India's quest for energy security; and contest with China for oil assets;
- Building new partnerships, and investing in stable, oil-rich countries like the US and Canada, while keeping up existing energy relations with Saudi Arabia, the UAE and Kuwait;
- Using market mechanisms to ensure energy security.

Topical and comprehensive, this book in *The Gateway House Guide to India in the 2020s series* will be useful for scholars and researchers of international relations, geopolitics, foreign policy, security and strategic studies, energy studies, West Asia studies, South Asian studies, and international trade. It will also be of interest to policymakers, diplomats, career bureaucrats, and professionals working with think tanks, academia and multilateral agencies, media agencies, and businesses.

Amit Bhandari is the Fellow for Energy and Environment Studies at Gateway House: Indian Council on Global Relations, India. His research encompasses India's energy security priorities and the role of financial markets, geopolitics, technology, and policy in achieving those goals. Amit has also studied China's Belt and Road Initiative and has authored papers studying Chinese Investments in South Asia and Chinese Investments in India.

Amit has nearly two decades of experience in covering financial and energy markets. He started his career with the *Economic Times*, where he tracked the energy sector. He was a part of the startup team of ET Now, the business news channel. Amit was responsible for setting up India Reality Research, a new research outfit within CLSA India, a stockbroking firm. He has also worked with the Deccan Chronicle Group as the business editor of their general dailies. He holds a Masters in Business Administration from the Indian Institute of Management, Ahmedabad, India and a Bachelors degree in Technology from the Institute of Technology, Benaras Hindu University, India.

The Gateway House Guide to India in the 2020s

Series Editor: **Manjeet Kripalani**, *co-founder, Gateway House: Indian Council on Global Relations*

The Gateway House Guide to India in the 2020s explores the connections between India's globalist past to the strengths it has developed as it steps into the future, starting with the decade of the 2020s. The volumes in this series discuss a wide range of topics, which include solutions for energy independence and environmental preservation, exposition of the new frontiers in space and technology, India's trade networks, security, foreign policies, and international relations. Furthermore, the series examines the embedded trading and entrepreneurial communities which are coming together to influence global agenda-setting and institution-building through platforms like the G20 and UN Security Council, where India will take leadership roles in this decade, in the Post-COVID-19 pandemic world.

This series appeals to an international audience, and is directed to policymakers, think tanks, bureaucrats, professionals working in the area of politics; scholars and researchers of political science, international relations, foreign policy, world economy, politics and technology, Asian politics, South Asia studies, and contemporary history; students and the general reader, seeking an understanding of what will drive India's positioning in world affairs.

Mercantile Bombay
A Journey of Trade, Finance and Enterprise
Sifra Lentin

India and the Changing Geopolitics of Oil
Amit Bhandari

For more information about this series, please visit:
https://www.routledge.com/The-Gateway-House-Guide-to-India-in-the-2020s/book-series/GHGI20

India and the Changing Geopolitics of Oil

Amit Bhandari

R Routledge
Taylor & Francis Group

LONDON AND NEW YORK

First published 2022
by Routledge
4 Park Square, Milton Park, Abingdon, Oxon OX14 4RN

and by Routledge
605 Third Avenue, New York, NY 10158

First issued in paperback 2023

Routledge is an imprint of the Taylor & Francis Group, an informa business

© 2022 Gateway House: Indian Council on Global Relations

British Library Cataloguing-in-Publication Data
A catalogue record for this book is available from the British Library

Library of Congress Cataloging-in-Publication Data
A catalog record has been requested for this book

ISBN: 978-0-367-64003-3 (hbk)
ISBN: 978-0-367-71613-4 (pbk)
ISBN: 978-1-003-15292-7 (ebk)

DOI: 10.4324/9781003152927

Typeset in Times New Roman
by codeMantra

Contents

Figures

Tables

1 Flux in the energy world
From peak oil to negative prices

April 2020 saw an unprecedented event in the world oil market – the price of West Texas Intermediate (WTI), one of the most widely traded benchmarks globally, fell to –**$36/barrel** as the April contracts neared expiry. Meaning, you had to pay your customer $36/barrel to take your oil away. Prices went negative because of the COVID-19 pandemic – global oil demand tanked by 30% in a matter of weeks while production continued at pre-crisis levels, leading to a glut of oil. Production from operational oil fields cannot be switched on or off like a tap, so fresh oil continued to reach the market. Dumping the oil is an environmental crime and not possible – so traders holding oil purchase contracts ended up paying large amounts to buyers willing to pick up this oil. Eventually, the US ran out of places to store this oil. Supertankers, which can carry up to 2 million barrels of oil, were chartered not to move the oil but to store it.

This is a complete about-turn compared with the early 2000s, when fears of peak oil were rife. As per the peak oil theory, the world oil production was set to reach a peak (2006 by some estimates), after which it would enter a terminal decline. The ever-reducing supply would keep pushing up prices, making abundant and affordable oil a thing of the past. Lacking cheap energy, poor countries like India would be forever stuck at lower incomes. Hundreds of books dealing with the subject and its various dimensions have been written. Luckily for us, it didn't happen. Google Trends shows that interest in peak oil peaked around 2005 and has since abated.

Peak oil was killed by a mix of supply- and demand-driven factors. World oil supply has increased and has become more diversified because of increasing production of unconventional oil, primarily shale-oil in the US and oil-sands of Canada. At the same time, oil demand

DOI: 10.4324/9781003152927-1

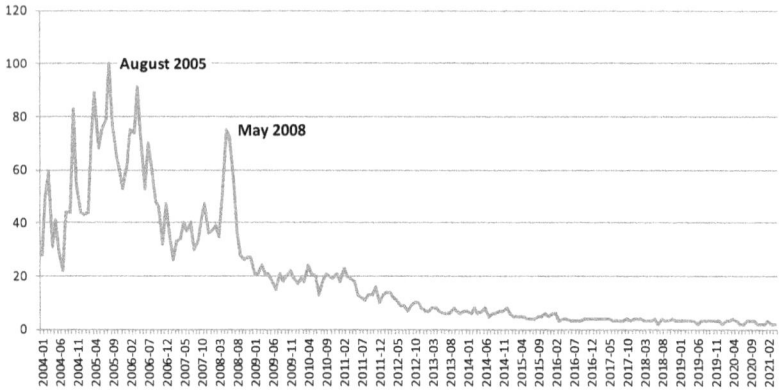

Figure 1.1 Peak Oil – No Longer Peaking

growth has slowed down – it has actually reversed in most of the high-income European countries and Japan – a mix of ageing population and improving energy efficiency. The increasing use of renewable energy, particularly electric vehicles, has also played a role. As a result, the focus is now on peak-demand – the point at which global oil demand will reach a peak and then start to decline. A lot of the known oil reserves are destined to never leave the ground. The April trade in WTI, precipitated by COVID-19, showed what happens when supply exceeds demand by a big margin.

Moreover, COVID-19 itself may become a long-term factor in shaping how energy markets develop. Early projections suggested that the global oil demand for 2020 would shrink by an unprecedented 8.1 million barrels per day[1] – almost 8% of all oil consumption. Not all of this will come back even as the world economy recovers. For instance, air travel – which constitutes an important part of oil consumption – may not recover to pre-COVID levels for years, if ever. Some of India's tech giants – such as TCS[2] and Infosys,[3] which employ hundreds of thousands of workers – may introduce permanent 'work from home' policies, so that only a small fraction of their staff needs to be physically present at the workplace, reducing the need for commutes. Workplaces have become used – for want of better options – to video-conferencing apps, which may also reduce the requirement for business travel in the long run. On the flip side, people may be more reluctant to use public transport and opt for personal vehicles, due to health concerns.

All of these trends have big implications for India, which is the world's third largest user and importer of oil, with a growing demand.

Saudi Arabia's bet

Peak oil turned out to be a bubble. Is peak-demand going to be the same? Many oil producers, who have the most to lose in such a scenario, are not betting on it. Saudi Arabia, which has, for decades, been the poster boy of a conservative, oil-fuelled monarchy, is trying to change, socially and economically, under the leadership of Crown Prince Muhammad bin Salman (MBS). The Vision 2030, a document first unveiled in 2016, speaks of diversifying the Saudi economy away from oil and converting the Kingdom into an investment powerhouse, Saudi Aramco into a global industrial giant and the Sovereign Wealth Fund (SWF) into the world's largest wealth fund.

It is not possible to change the economic base of the country without also changing the society. Thus, social liberalism goes hand in hand with economic liberalism. In 2019, Saudi Arabia cut down gender segregation in public places, finally allowed women to drive cars and permitted music concerts – hitherto banned. On the economic front, the Kingdom is promoting a new finance hub – the King Abdullah Economic City as well as other cities being set up for entertainment and tourism. One of the biggest projects is a city called Neom, on the northern Red Sea coast of the Kingdom, which will function as a smart city and a tourism hub.

To fund these new investments/diversifications, the Kingdom announced it will be listing its prime asset – Saudi Aramco, the national oil company. First talked about in 2016, the IPO was projected to raise $100 billion for the Kingdom, enabling new investments.[4] The IPO was temporarily shelved and then scaled down by almost 70% – eventually to a still massive $25.4 billion for 1.5% shares in the company.[5] Post IPO, Aramco has become the most valuable company in the world – worth $1.7 trillion at its IPO price and touching $2 trillion as well in the weeks following the IPO.

One of the reasons for the Aramco IPO was to create a kitty for future investments, many of them to be made via the SWF of the Kingdom. This SWF has made large investments in Uber and Tesla, two of the best-known start-ups globally,[6] and with business models that can dramatically alter the global energy demand scenario, and Saudi Arabia's fortunes. Saudi Arabia is clearly trying to hedge its bets against a future where oil may no longer be central to the fortunes of the world economy. Saudi Arabia's caution is warranted – major trends are under way that may reshape the global energy scenario.

Oil demand: from West to Asia

The two most closely followed numbers in the oil world are the prices of Brent and WTI. Brent is the name for the light, sweet crude produced from a North-Sea oil field owned by Royal Dutch Shell. Over time, it has become the most closely followed benchmark for pricing of oil contracts, much like how Libor is used to set interest rates in financial contracts. Other oils are priced at a certain discount (or premium, as the case may be) to the prevailing price of Brent crude. Production from the Brent field first began in 1976 – the field is currently being decommissioned.[7] WTI is an even older benchmark, with price records going back to over 70 years. Like Brent, WTI is also a light, sweet crude. Unlike Brent, it doesn't come from a single field but is a blend of oils from several fields.

The two most important historical oil benchmarks are both Western crude oils, simply because for most of the recorded oil age, the West has been the largest consumer of oil. In 1973, the year of the first oil-shock, seven of the top eight oil consumers were either the US or its allies. India didn't even figure in the top ten users of oil. Countries such as Sweden and Belgium – which have populations less than half of India's major metros such as Mumbai and Delhi – consumed more oil than all of India at that time.

And how things have changed! India is now the third largest user of oil, and its oil consumption has gone up more than tenfold – consuming as much oil as Germany, France and the UK combined! China's oil consumption has increased in a similar manner – it is now the second largest consumer of oil after the US. Over the same period, Western countries such as Japan, Germany and France have seen their oil consumption decline – a mix of improved energy efficiency, ageing populations and greater use of renewable energy. Because of this shift, China had displaced the US as the world's largest oil importer. India comes in at the third place. Thus, the oil trade, which was earlier from the Middle East to the West, is now shifting to the East.

Table 1.1 Major Oil Consumers: Then and Now

	1973	2018
USA	17,318	20,456
USSR	5,981	3,228 (Russian Federation)
Japan	5,265	3,854
Germany	3,249	2,321
France	2,499	1,607
UK	2,228	1,618
Italy	1,983	1,253
Canada	1,682	2,447
China	1,058	13,525
India	474	5,516
World	55,658	99,843

Figures in 000 barrels/day.
Source: BP Statistical Review of World Energy.

Oil (and energy) demand of Asian countries, such as India, is going to increase further, while consumption in Europe (and West, in general) is going to decline due to the following two factors:

1 **Higher growth:** Because of its lower base (income), the Indian economy will grow much faster than the world average for many years to come. In 2019, the IMF projected India's 2020–2024 GDP growth at over 7%, despite a slowdown. Over the same period, the world economic output is projected to grow at just over 3%. Faster economic growth will power increased consumption, including the consumption of energy. While the COVID-19 pandemic may slow down India's growth, the long-term trend will still be upward.
2 **Youthful Population:** India's median age is 27.9 years (2018 estimate). In comparison, the median age of China is 37.4 years, while the US comes in at 38.1 years. Both Germany and Japan are over 45 years. Ageing population is an indication of lower fertility rates and will eventually result in reduced populations and reduced consumption of resources, including energy.

Oil supply shift: from Middle East to North America

From 2008 to 2018, the global oil production rose by 11.65 million bpd. Remarkably, most of this increase came not from Saudi Arabia or Venezuela, which have the world's largest reserves of oil. Almost three-fourths of this increase – an astonishing 8.5 million barrels per day – has come from the US (Table 1.2). Iraq and Canada added over

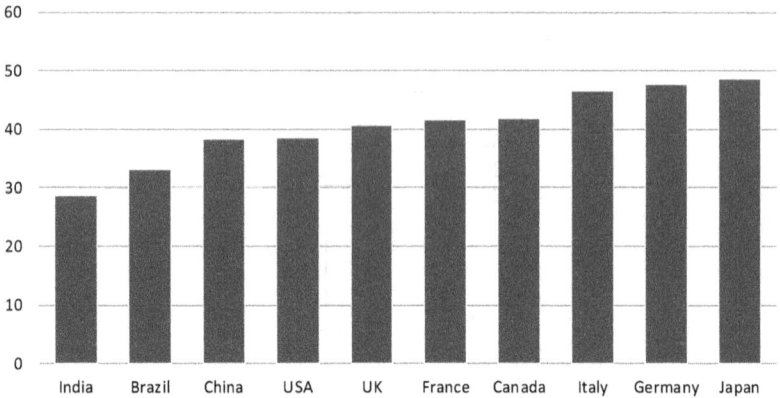

Figure 1.2 Median Age of Ten Largest Economies

Table 1.2 Ten-year Change in Oil Production

	2018 Oil Production	*Ten-year Change*
USA	15,311	8,527
Iraq	4,614	2,186
Canada	5,208	2,001
Saudi Arabia	12,287	1,622
Russian Federation	11,438	1,473
UAE	3,942	829
Kazakhstan	1,927	442
Iran	4,715	300
Kuwait	3,049	267
Venezuela	1,514	–1,712
World	**94,718**	**11,649**

Figures in thousand barrels/day.

Source: BP Statistical Review of World Energy.

2 million bpd of production each. Over the same period, Venezuela, which has the world's largest reserves of oil, saw its production decline by over 50%. News reports indicated that Venezuela's oil production in 2018 was the lowest since 1990.[8] Other oil exporters such as Nigeria, Angola and Algeria – all members of OPEC – have also seen decline in oil production over the past decade.

Oil-shale and oil-sands

The increased oil production from the US and Canada has come from oil-shale and oil-sands, respectively – two of the most expensive to extract forms of oil. Shale-oil refers to hydrocarbons trapped in impermeable rock, which must be extracted through an energy and water-intensive process called hydro-fracking or just fracking. Water, along with chemicals, is injected into wells at a high pressure, fracturing the rocks and allowing the trapped oil (or gas) to escape. Oil-sands are a form of viscous oil (bitumen) mixed with sand, clay and water. At normal temperatures, bitumen will not flow and needs to be either mixed with light oils or heated to liquefy it. Oil can be extracted from oil-sands either by mining the rock (much like coal) and then removing the oil or by injecting steam into the ground so that the oil can flow out. Conventional oil is much easier to produce – it either flows out of the ground on its own pressure or is brought out by pumping water (or carbon dioxide) into old wells where the pressure has fallen off.

As a result, oil shale and oil-sands are the most expensive forms of oil to produce. Extracting oil from these two resources is also more energy (carbon)-intensive, and therefore more polluting, an ever-growing concern. Historically, it was financially unviable to produce oil from either of the two sources.

Two factors changed that. High price of oil, starting from 2004 to 2014, often over $100 per barrel, made oil exploration more profitable. The high price also directed more effort into technical innovations in extracting oil from known, but financially unviable resources – since the payoffs were now so high. Big leaps were made in extracting gas and oil from shale, at progressively lower costs. This has eventually resulted in an extra 8.5 million bpd of oil supply.

Swing producer: Saudi to shale

Historically, Saudi Arabia has been the swing oil producer globally. If oil supply was tight and prices high, it could produce more oil. If oil supplies were plentiful and prices too low, it would cut down production. This is made possible by the spare capacity Saudi Aramco maintains – over 2 million bpd – developed at a cost of tens of billions of dollars and kept as a reserve. No other country/company can afford to invest such an amount and then let the investment idle.

This role too is now shifting to shale-oil producers in the US. A traditional oil well can remain in production for years and decades. Shale wells do most of their production within a week of drilling and have a life of a few weeks or months. It is also considerably cheaper (and takes less time) to drill a shale well. As a result, shale-oil producers can respond to market signals (price) faster. If prices start moving up too much, more wells will be drilled. In the case of low prices, drilling of new wells can be reduced, and production automatically responds to lower prices. As a result, Saudi Arabia is no longer able to dictate the price of oil by cutting/increasing production, as it was in the past.

Growing role of natural gas

A common sight in oil fields in the old days used to be large flames on top of oil rigs – this was natural gas being flared. At that time, gas was an undesirable and flammable waste product, which had to be disposed of – it is now a valuable product in its own right.

Natural gas is similar to crude oil in origin, and somewhat different in molecular structure. Crude oil is a mixture of hydrocarbons – chains of carbon atoms with hydrogen atoms attached to these chains. Natural gas is largely methane, a single carbon atom with four hydrogen atoms attached to it. Compared to other petroleum compounds, natural gas has less carbon; therefore, burning natural gas releases less carbon dioxide compared to other petroleum fuels. Other pollutants such as sulfur can also be removed entirely from natural gas before use, unlike oil. Therefore, natural gas is a preferred fuel in the rich world, at the expense of 'dirty' fuels such as coal. Natural gas is also pitched as a 'bridge fuel' – to be used as the world economy transitions from fossil fuels to clean energy. Globally, natural gas accounted for 23.9% of all energy consumed in 2019 – close to the share of coal. In India, however, natural gas had a share of just 6.2% in the energy mix.

Apart from its smaller carbon footprint, natural gas is also a way to reduce oil dependence. Natural gas, in the form of CNG, is used to power over 3 million vehicles in Delhi, Mumbai and Gujarat and is a direct replacement for petrol and diesel. India imports natural gas from Qatar, Australia and even the US – not India's traditional energy suppliers. Widening the supplier base automatically reduces supplier risk. Moreover, Australia and the US are stable democracies – they don't face instability that is common to oil-rich countries in West Asia, Africa and South America.

More gas discoveries in recent years mean that the pool of gas suppliers is going to be even wider. For instance, major gas discoveries have been made offshore Mozambique (Rovuma Basin), Israel (Leviathan gas field) and Egypt (Zohr). Mozambique and Israel are likely to become LNG exporters in the near future. Another potential player in the gas market is Argentina – which has 11.1 trillion cubic feet of conventional gas reserves but has 310 trillion cubic feet[9] (equivalent to 51 billion barrels of oil) of unconventional gas – similar to the US shale. In 2019, Argentina exported its first ever cargo of LNG.[10] While it is currently a marginal player, Argentina can also become a major gas supplier in the future.

Table 1.3 Top LNG Exporters

	2019 Exports	Market Share (%)
Qatar	77.8	22%
Australia	75.4	21%
USA	33.8	10%
Russia	29.3	8%
Malaysia	26.2	7%
Figures in million tons/year		

Source: World LNG Report, 2020.

Due to these factors, natural gas will play a larger role in India's energy mix. India's domestic reserves of natural gas, like oil, are very limited – meaning any increase in consumption can only be met via imports.

However, unlike oil, natural gas cannot be just loaded on to a ship and moved where needed. There are two ways to transport natural gas. The first is via cross-country pipelines. The US, for instance, has an extensive pipeline network for moving natural gas from where it is produced to where it is needed. Russia, the world's largest gas producer, has been exporting natural gas to Western Europe via long-distance pipelines for decades. India has also tried to replicate this and import gas from its energy-rich neighbours – specifically Iran and Turkmenistan. However, adverse geopolitics – specifically Pakistan, which will have to be crossed by these pipelines – means that these pipelines are unlikely to materialise in the foreseeable future.

The other way to transport natural gas is to cool it to 160 degrees Celsius below the freezing point of water, at which the gas becomes a liquid occupying a small volume and easy to move. However, expensive infrastructure is required to cool the gas to liquid, special ships are required to move the supercool gas and then special infrastructure is again needed to convert the liquid to gas. India's first LNG terminal was built at Dabhol – to import gas for the infamous Dabhol Power Plant. However, controversies linked to the Dabhol Power Project ensured that the project didn't become operational for over a decade. The first operational terminal was completed in 2002 in Dahej, Gujarat, by Petronet LNG – a special purpose company created to build LNG terminals. Since then, four more LNG terminals have come up with more terminals in the pipeline. Similar to oil, the issue with natural gas is not its availability, but the price at which it is available. LNG prices move in line with oil prices, so it is the same challenge – adequate supplies at an affordable price.

From fossil fuels to renewable

Oil, natural gas and coal account for almost 85% of the total energy consumption worldwide. The remainder comes from hydropower, nuclear energy and, increasingly, renewable energy. During 2018, renewable energy (solar, wind energy) accounted for 4% of world energy mix, the highest ever. India has also announced an ambitious target of 175 GW of renewable energy capacity by 2022.[11] By 2022, India is projected to have 479 GW of power generation capacity, of which 36.5% will be from renewable sources, primarily solar and wind farms. From 2022 to 2027, another 100 GW of renewable energy capacity is projected to be added to the Indian power grid. These large numbers are a part of India's commitment to deal with Anthropogenic (manmade) Climate Change – a global issue, and urban air pollution, a local problem.

From the beginning of the industrial age, humanity has consumed ever-increasing amounts of fossil fuels – coal, oil and then natural gas. This has caused an increase in the amount of carbon dioxide in the earth's atmosphere. Carbon dioxide is one of the gases that trap solar heat and lead to global warming, an increase in the earth's temperature. This is termed as Anthropogenic Climate Change. A detailed discussion of climate change and global warming is beyond the scope of this book. Our concern here is with the energy choices that India has made. One set of choices, on renewable energy, is being increasingly driven by climate change concerns.

BOX 1.1 CAN RENEWABLE ENERGY SCALE UP?

As it reaches a critical mass, renewable energy (solar and wind) is now coming up against a major barrier that may prevent its widespread adoption – the bankruptcy of buyers. Most of India's electricity distribution in India is carried out by state utilities, which often have their generation arms. These utilities are also in a financial black hole.

In 2015–2016, 24% of all electricity was not paid for – it is called Aggregate Technical and Commercial (AT&C) losses, or theft. This share of generation generates no revenue. Another 22% goes to the agricultural sector, often free or at much lower than cost – collectively, this generates only 8% of the revenue. With almost half of their production not getting any revenue, the state power utilities are in a financial hole, and they are collectively bankrupt.

They cannot afford anything other than the cheapest electricity coming from the oldest coal-fired power plants. As a result, existing renewable energy purchases are being hurt. Tamil Nadu has a large installed base of wind turbines. However, during the monsoon, when wind energy generation is maximum, the state electricity board finds it cheaper to purchase electricity from coal-fired power plants than from these windmills. The windmills turn useless. The other problem renewable energy is now facing is renegotiation of old contracts. The Andhra government has tried to renegotiate renewable energy purchase contracts which they have signed earlier, when renewable energy costs were higher and required larger financial outlay. Renegotiation of contracts will scare away investors in the future.

The other big environmental concern in India is the increasingly poor air quality across major Indian cities. One study by AirVisual indicates that 15 of the 20 most polluted cities (by PM 2.5 content in air) are in India.[12] The air quality in Delhi is routinely in the hazardous range during the winter months, when a smog engulfs Northern India. This is a mix of smoke from India's coal-fired power plants, vehicles and construction dust, which are generated all year round, made worse by farmers burning stubble to clear their fields. During the rest of the year, warm air from the surface rises, taking these pollutants away. However, during the winter, this smog forms a layer of cool air close to the surface and doesn't dissipate. Shifting from the internal combustion engine to electric vehicles could be one way to clean up the air in Indian cities.

Electric vehicles

An electric vehicle, as the name implies, runs on an electric motor – like a ceiling fan or any other electric motor. Instead of a fuel tank, these vehicles need a battery. Electric vehicles are far more energy-efficient compared to petrol/diesel vehicles – as an electric motor has very few moving parts compared to an internal combustion engine, so more of the energy gets converted to motive power. Thus, the ten most energy-efficient cars in the US are all electric,[13] with a fuel efficiency of over 100 miles/gallon (42 km/L). This is at least twice the mileage given by the most energy-efficient car with an IC engine. Fewer moving parts also mean less need for servicing and spares, bringing down ownership costs.

Electric cars such as Tesla have captured popular imagination and are popular in the higher end of the market. Worldwide electric car

sales in 2019 were 2.2 million, 2.5% of all cars sold that year.[14] While electric vehicles still have a long way to go, with sales of over 2 million and growing, they are clearly no longer a cottage industry, but a serious alternative to the internal combustion engine. The Niti Aayog, a body that advises the Indian government, has argued in favour of electric mobility, especially electric two-wheelers in the past.[15] Niti Aayog has been extensively quoted in the Indian media as having said that post-2030, only electric vehicles will be permitted to be sold in the Indian market.[16]
There are two questions here:

- Can electric vehicles make a serious dent in the global oil demand?
- Can electric vehicles become widespread in India?

It seems unlikely at this point.

Electric vehicles require three key materials – lithium for batteries, cobalt for electrodes and rare-earth minerals for the motor. Lithium is a key component in a Lithium-ion battery, which is used to power most electric vehicles. Global lithium production in 2018 was 85,000 tons – the lithium requirement for one Tesla car is 7 kg[17] – so the current production has to be scaled up multiple times just to service the car market. With other vehicles – two-wheelers and trucks, the requirement will go up even further. Whether the lithium supply chain can scale up by 10–20× to meet this requirement is uncertain. Moreover, two-thirds of the existing lithium production comes from a single source – Australia.

There is a similar concentration in other raw materials – rare earths and cobalt.

Table 1.4 Lithium Reserves and Production 2018

	Production (tons)	*Reserves (tons)*
Argentina	6,200	2,000,000
Australia	**51,000**	**2,700,000**
Bolivia	–	–
Brazil	600	54,000
Chile	16,000	8,000,000
China	8,000	1,000,000
Portugal	800	60,000
Namibia	500	–
Zimbabwe	1,600	70,000
US	SECRET	35,000
World	**85,000**	**14,000,000**

Source: BP Statistical Review.

Rare earths is the name given to a group of 17 metallic elements in the periodic table, many of which were discovered in the small town of Ytterby in Sweden and four elements are named after this one town. Some of these minerals are used to make powerful magnets – which are used in earphones and also electric motors – making them a key component of electric vehicles. In 2018, China accounted for two-thirds of all rare-earth production globally. In the past, China has used its control of the rare-earth supply chain as a political tool – most notably against Japan in 2010 during a maritime dispute. China has also imposed restrictions on exports of rare-earth minerals, to force foreign firms to set up high-tech manufacturing facilities in China. This particular dispute was resolved by the WTO in 2014,[18] against China. However, China has in the past disregarded international conventions. It cannot be guaranteed that China will not use its control of the rare-earth supply chain as a political tool.

There is a similar issue for the third leg of the EV supply chain – cobalt, a high-density metallic element, needed for lithium-ion batteries. In 2018, 70% of the world's cobalt production came from the Democratic Republic of Congo, which suffers political unrest and civil strife. Worse, news reports indicate that 8 of the 14 cobalt mining companies in the DRC are now owned/controlled by Chinese companies.[19]

Table 1.5 Rare Earth Production and Reserves 2018

	Production (000 tons)	*Reserves (000 tons)*
China	120	44,000
Australia	18.6	3,400
US	15	1,400
Rest of the World	13.1	67,000
World	166.7	116,749

Source: BP Statistical Review

Table 1.6 Cobalt Reserves and Production 2018

	Production (000 tons)	*Reserves (000 tons)*
DR Congo	111.7	3,400
Russia	5.9	250
Philippines	4.4	280
Australia	4.7	1,200
Cuba	4.5	500
Rest of the World	26.9	939
World	158.1	6,569

Source: BP Statistical Review

The world oil supply chain has proven itself over the past 70 years. It has delivered during wars, civil strife and natural disasters. No single buyer or supplier controls a large pie of this market. In contrast, the EV supply chain relies on three minerals – all of which come from a single source, a recipe for disaster. In the case of two of these minerals – rare earths and cobalt, the sources are not the most reliable. Moreover, these supply chains will have to scale up manifold – by 25–50×, if electric vehicles are to expand beyond 1% of the car market.

BOX 1.2 CAN CHINA BE TRUSTED WITH A RARE-EARTH MONOPOLY?

The Senkakus are a group of uninhabited Japanese islands, which have been Japanese territory since 1895.[20] Since the 1970s, the People's Republic of China has also laid claim to these islands, citing historical documents.[21] China has expansive claims against virtually all its maritime neighbours including the Philippines, Vietnam, Malaysia and Indonesia. In many of these cases, China relies on People's Armed Forces Maritime Militia (PAFMM). PAFMM is the only government-sanctioned maritime militia in the world with hundreds of 'fishing' boats – with reinforced hulls and compartments to store ammunition.[22] PAFMM boats routinely go in large numbers to disputed waters, in an attempt to challenge control and change facts on the ground, without bringing in the formal armed forces. Many of these fishing boats get involved in 'accidents' and collisions with foreign navies.

Chinese fishing boats routinely intrude into the waters around Senkaku islands, which are Japanese maritime territory and is patrolled by the Japanese coast guard. In September 2010, a Chinese fishing boat was within these waters and was challenged by the Japanese coast guard. While attempting to flee, this boat collided with a Japanese coast guard vessel. The captain and the crew of this vessel were detained. This led to a major diplomatic showdown between China and Japan. At one point, China stopped exports of rare earths to Japan. Rare earth minerals such as neodymium and dysprosium are used in making compact electronics such as touch-phones, high-power earphones, etc.

From the 1990s, China accounted for an ever-increasing share of the global rare-earth production, going up to 95% by 2009.

Mines elsewhere in the world, including the US, shut down as it was cheaper to buy from China rather than produce in-house. Therefore, it wasn't possible for Japanese companies to source the materials from elsewhere. From that time, corporations have tried to diversify the base of rare-earth supplies, but China still accounts for over two-thirds of the global rare earth production. Can it be considered a reliable supplier given its geopolitical ambitions and disputes with its neighbours?

Renewable energy

India's ambitious renewable energy target of 175 GW by 2022 has two major drivers:

- India's own environmental commitments
- Falling prices of renewable energy

Solar power is going to account for the bulk of this new capacity (57%, 100 GW) while wind energy will be the bulk of the remaining capacity (60 GW, 34%). Overall, renewable energy will account for 36% of India's installed power generation capacity. As of September 2019, India's installed renewable energy capacity was 82.5 GW.[23] Compared to thermal, hydro and nuclear power, the installation time for solar/wind projects is much smaller – less than 2-years versus anywhere from 3 to 10 years. Another advantage of renewable energy is that it is modular. A 1,000-MW nuclear power plant cannot generate a single unit of electricity till all of it is complete. A 1,000-MW solar farm doesn't need to wait for the full project to get over before generating electricity, and therefore it is much more efficient with capital.

However, these numbers overstate the role renewable energy will play (and is playing) in the Indian energy scenario. There are still some unaddressed issues:

- **Lower capacity utilisation:** The sun shines only for part of 24-hours, and wind blows intermittently. Therefore, 1 MW of solar/wind power produces much less electricity compared to 1 MW of coal/nuclear power. Thus, even though renewable power may account for 36% of installed power generation capacity, its share of actual electricity produced will be less than half that.

- **Intermittency and lack of storage options:** There is no control over when renewable power gets generated. As a result, electricity must be stored when it is being generated, to be used when it is needed. As of now, there are no viable grid-scale power storage solutions available in India.
- **Bankruptcy of SEBs:** The bulk (over 90%) of the electricity produced in India is bought by state utilities – the State Electricity Boards – which then supply this to end consumers. About 20% of all electricity generated in India is stolen, and a similar share is sold to the farm sector at a fraction of cost. As a result, the SEBs in India are collectively bankrupt. If the largest group of customers is bankrupt, financing new capital investment will be difficult.

Because of these three factors, renewable energy is likely to play a limited role in India's energy mix.

Market power shift: from seller to buyer

As a result of these factors – the changing patterns of oil demand and supply, and the increased use of renewable energy/electric vehicles, market power is shifting from the sellers to the buyers. This shift marks a reversal of the process that started in 1973 with the oil-shock.

As a result of shale-oil and oil-sands, there is no shortage of oil. If prices move up, production can ramp up to meet the demand quickly. Oil demand is slowing down due to a mix of ageing populations, increasing efficiency and use of technologies such as RE/EV. As a result, there is enough oil but fewer buyers. Just as oil buyers used to worry about security of supplies, oil exporters are now worried about demand security.

India, with its already large and fast-growing demand for oil is a major source of demand security for oil exporters. This can be seen from the increasing importance India gets in West Asia, home to Saudi Arabia, Iraq, Kuwait and Abu Dhabi. This is the reason Saudi Arabia and India signed a Strategic Partnership Council Agreement in October 2019, during Prime Minister Modi's visit to the Kingdom. Saudi Arabia has identified India as one of its eight strategic partners and is also looking at investing in Indian petroleum refining and retail businesses. Saudi Aramco has two major investment proposals in India – it is a partner in the proposed 60-million-ton West Coast Refinery, and it may acquire a 20% stake in the petroleum business of Reliance Industries.

Saudi Arabia is not the only oil exporter interested in India. Russia's Rosneft acquired the 20-million-ton refinery in Vadinar from Essar Oil – now called Nayara Energy, even though Russia doesn't export much oil to India. Indian government-owned oil companies are invested heavily in several Russian oil fields – which couldn't have happened without the approval of the Russian government. India's ONGC has also invested in oil fields in Abu Dhabi, again requiring government approval. Abu Dhabi National Oil Company (ADNOC) is also a partner in the West Coast Refinery project.

India is being wooed by major oil and gas producers across the world. It needs to use this newfound status to secure its interests.

Notes

1 IEA. 2020. "Oil Market Report – June 2020". IEA. Paris. https://www.iea. org/reports/oil-market-report-june-2020
2 Financial Express. 2020. "TCS 'Work from Home' Policy: Only One-Fourth of Workers to Come to Office; CEO Explains Vision 25×25." *The Financial Express*, May 27, 2020. https://www.financialexpress.com/ industry/tcs-work-from-home-policy-only-one-fourth-of-workers-to-come-to-office-ceo-explains-vision-25x25/1971995/#:~:text=One%20 of%20India
3 Malik, Bismah. 2020. "Infosys to Introduce Permanent 'Flexible Work from Home Model' for Employees." *The New Indian Express*, June 27, 2020. https://www.newindianexpress.com/business/2020/jun/27/infosys-to-introduce-permanent-flexible-work-from-home-model-for-employees-2162275.html
4 Kalin, Rania El and Stephen Gamal. 2017. "Exclusive: Saudi Aramco IPO on Track for 2018 – Saudi Crown Prince." *Reuters*, October 26, 2017. https:// in.reuters.com/article/saudi-aramco-ipo-crownprince/exclusive-saudi-aramco-ipo-on-track-for-2018-saudi-crown-prince-idINKBN1CV2MV
5 Saudi Aramco. 2019. "Saudi Arabian Oil Company (Saudi Aramco): Listed on Tadawul." https://www.saudiaramco.com/-/media/images/investors/saudi-aramco-listed-on-tadawul.pdf?la=en&hash=A83C89668C3B94B5E C963ADAAD765910E40356EA
6 Arabian Business. 2020. "Saudi Arabia's Public Investment Fund Parts Ways with Three Executives." https://www.arabianbusiness.com/banking-finance/442068-saudi-arabias-public-investment-fund-parts-ways-with-th ree-executives
7 Shell UK. n.d. "Top 5 Questions about Brent." www.shell.co.uk. https://www.shell.co.uk/sustainability/decommissioning/brent-field-decommissioning/top-5-questions-about-brent.html
8 Kassai, Lucia. 2019. "Venezuela Oil Exports Slump to a 28-Year Low." *Bloomberg.com*, January 2, 2019. https://www.bloomberg.com/news/ articles/2019-01-02/venezuela-oil-exports-slump-to-28-year-low-on-falling-output

9 Clemente, Jude. 2019. "Argentina Primed for Great Natural Gas Rise." www. rigzone.com. October 16, 2019. https://www.rigzone.com/news/argentina_primed_for_great_natural_gas_rise-16-oct-2019-160071-article/

10 Slav, Irina. 2019. "Argentina Exports First-Ever Cargo of LNG." OilPrice. com. June 3, 2019. https://oilprice.com/Latest-Energy-News/World-News/Argentina-Exports-First-Ever-Cargo-Of-LNG.html

11 Ministry of New and Renewable Energy, Government of India. "Power Production through Energy Sources." Lok Sabha. Question no. 372. 2019. http://164.100.24.220/loksabhaquestions/annex/171/AS372.pdf

12 IQAir. n.d. "World's Most Polluted Cities in 2019 – PM2.5 Ranking | AirVisual." www.iqair.com. Accessed March 5, 2021. https://www.airvisual.com/world-most-polluted-cities?continent=&country=&state=&page=1&perPage=50&cities=

13 U.S. Department of Energy. n.d. "Fueleconomy.gov Top Ten." www. fueleconomy.gov. Accessed March 5, 2021. https://www.fueleconomy.gov/feg/topten.jsp?year=2020&action=All

14 https://insideevs.com/news/396177/global-ev-sales-december-2019/

15 NITI Aayog & World Energy Council. 2018. "Zero Emission Vehicles (ZEVs): Towards a Policy Framework." https://niti.gov.in/writereaddata/files/document_publication/EV_report.pdf

16 Firstpost. 2019. "Only Electric Vehicles to Be Sold after 2030 Says NITI Aayog in Its Latest Proposal-Technology News, Firstpost." *Tech2*, June 18, 2019. https://www.firstpost.com/tech/news-analysis/only-electric-vehicles-to-be-sold-after-2030-says-niti-aayog-in-its-latest-proposal-6835331.html

17 Researchgate. "What Is the Content of Pure Lithium (E.g. Kg/KWh) in Li-Ion Batteries Used in Electric Vehicles?" ResearchGate. https://www.researchgate.net/post/What_is_the_content_of_pure_lithium_eg_kg_kWh_in_Li-ion_batteries_used_in_electric_vehicles

18 Appellate Body Report. "China- Measures Related to the Exportation of Rare Earths, Tungsten and Molybdenum." WTO doc #: 14-4626. Adopted: 29 August 2014.

19 Farchy, Jack, and Hayley Warren. 2019. "Cobalt Control: China's Secret Weapon in the Race to Dominate Electric Car Industry." Independent.ie. Independent.ie, April 5, 2019. https://www.independent.ie/business/world/cobalt-control-chinas-secret-weapon-in-the-race-to-dominate-electric-car-industry-37984215.html

20 Ministry of Foreign Affairs of Japan. 2014. "Situation of the Senkaku Islands." https://www.mofa.go.jp/a_o/c_m1/senkaku/page1we_000010.html

21 Diaoyu Dao. n.d. "Diaoyu Dao_Diaoyu Dao: The Inherent Territory of China." http://www.diaoyudao.org.cn/en/index.htm

22 Office of the Secretary of Defense. 2018. "Military and Security Developments Involving the People's Republic of China 2018." Department of Defense. https://media.defense.gov/2018/Aug/16/2001955282/-1/-1/1/2018-CHINA-MILITARY-POWER-REPORT.PDF

23 Central Electricity Authority, Government of India. 2019. "Executive Summary on Power Sector, September 2019." https://cea.nic.in/old/reports/monthly/executivesummary/2019/exe_summary-09.pdf

2 India's quest for energy security

India has depended on imported oil from the beginning of oil age, during the British era. At the time of independence, the only significant oil fields in India were in Assam. Oil imports were a major drain on India's balance of payments, and the government wanted to prioritise oil exploration. Therefore, it set up the Oil & Natural Gas Commission in 1956, to *"plan, promote, organize and implement programmes for development of Petroleum Resources and the production and sale of petroleum and petroleum products produced by it, and to perform such other functions as the Central Government may, from time to time, assign to it."* This, later on, became the Oil & Natural Gas Corporation and is now just ONGC Limited. ONGC made significant discoveries in the Cambay Basin and in the giant Bombay High oil field. However, these discoveries covered only a part of India's oil needs. Post liberalisation in the early 1990s, India also tried to encourage the private sector in oil exploration. The two big successes here were the onshore oil fields in Rajasthan, discovered by Cairn and the offshore gas fields in the KG Basin, discovered by the Reliance-Niko joint venture.

Over this period, India's dependence on imported oil has continued to increase – from 33% in 1990–1991[1] to 85% in 2019.[2] The import dependence reduced during the 1980s because of the Bombay High discovery but has since been on an upward trend.

The high dependence on imported oil has led to an unfortunate relationship with high oil prices – whenever oil prices have gone up sharply, India has suffered. The oil shocks of the 1970s hurt the Indian economy badly while 1991 brought it to the brink.

Oil shocks – 1973 and 1979

Following the Arab–Israel war of 1973, the Organization of Arab Petroleum Exporting Countries (OAPEC) declared an embargo on oil exports to countries they perceived as supporting Israel. This included the US,

DOI: 10.4324/9781003152927-2

the Netherlands, Portugal and South Africa.[3] The embargo banned exports of raw petroleum and petroleum products such as diesel and petrol to these countries. However, oil is a fungible commodity. It can be purchased from multiple sources – enforcing the embargo also meant production cuts, and therefore price increases. By March 1974, the price of oil had gone up almost four times to $12/barrel from $3/barrel pre-embargo.

India was an oil importer even in the 1970s, and the high prices hurt in multiple ways. India's oil import bill from April to September 1974 was Rs 586 crore – versus just Rs 152 crore for the same period in the preceding year. The increase in import bill was due to higher prices of oil. There was a steep increase in fertiliser import bill as well – from Rs 78 crore to Rs 194 crore – petroleum products like naphtha and natural gas are inputs for fertiliser production as well. India's foodgrain imports also increased due to poor harvest, and because of high input (fertiliser) prices, food prices were also higher.[4] The Economic Survey for the year describes 1974–1975 as one *"of unprecedented economic strains in the history of independent India"*.[5] The fiscal year 1974–1975 saw the Indian economy grow by just 1%.[6]

The second oil shock in the 1980s also had its origins in West Asia. In 1979, the Shah of Iran was finally deposed by the Islamic Revolution, and Iran, which produced 5.3 million barrels/day of oil in 1978 (8% of the world production), saw its production fall by nearly three-fourths by 1981. The supply shock, coupled with fears of further unrest in other oil producers resulted in a tripling in the price of oil[7] – touching $40/barrel, a level not again seen till 2004. India again was among the worst sufferers. The Indian economy *shrank* by an unprecedented 4.8%.[8]

Third oil shock: 1991 balance of payment's crisis

India's third external shock, much worse than the first two, also arose from the Gulf. In August 1990, Iraq's Dictator Saddam Hussein attacked and annexed Kuwait. Iraq claimed multiple reasons for the attack:

- Iraq had just come out of a long war with Iran, financed by debt from the UAE and Kuwait, which the two refused to write off
- Iraq alleged that Kuwait was 'stealing' oil from a shared oil field on their border
- Sovereignty dispute over two islands owned by Kuwait. At the time of Kuwait's independence, Iraq had refused to recognise the latter, claiming it was a part of the Ottoman province of Al-Basrah.[9]

The Iraqi army overran Kuwait in a short time and declared it Iraq's nineteenth province. The United Nations refused to recognise Iraq's actions and imposed sanctions. Ultimately, a US-led and UN-sanctioned coalition army beat back the Iraqi army and restored Kuwait's sovereignty in what was called the Gulf War.

Meanwhile, the price of oil shot up. From an average of $287 million/month in June–August 1990, India's oil import bill shot up to an average of $671 million/month for the next 6 months (from September 1990 to February 1991). What made the crisis worse for India this time was the fall in remittance income. Millions of Indians work in Gulf and their remittances are an important source of forex for India. A large number of workers based in Kuwait had to be evacuated and remittances ceased. In January 1991, India's total forex reserves had fallen to $896 million – not sufficient to cover a month of imports. India was at risk of defaulting on its external obligations, for the first time.

Eventually, the Indian government had to take a step that shocked the Indian psyche – 20 tons of India's gold reserves were sold and another 47 tons of gold was pledged with the Bank of England to raise funds.[10] This shock paved the way for India's economic reforms and subsequent growth.

India's search for equity oil

The years 1973, 1979 and 1991 showed India's vulnerability to high oil prices. One way to cut down this dependence is to increase domestic production. India tried to do this via ONGC, but oil discovery depends on much more than efforts, and given India's geology, it is clear that this is not an approach that will work for the country. Apart from poor geological prospects, there are other problems of doing business in India as well, which will keep away foreign oil companies. In 2014, Cairn India was slapped with a $1.6 billion retrospective tax claim for a restructuring carried out by the company in 2006.[11] The Indian fuel retail market worked under a quasi-APM from 2005 to 2015, where companies lost money on retail sales – with government making up those losses – but only for the public sector, driving private sector fuel retailers out of business. Large-scale land acquisition is another problem. Any global oil company can tap better geological prospects where it is easier to do business in preference to India. Thus, India's dependence on imported oil is unlikely to reduce meaningfully.

If you don't have oil fields of your own, the next best option is to acquire oil fields elsewhere – as Western oil majors have been doing for decades. However, the Western oil majors were all privately owned firms, while Indian oil companies were owned by the government. In practical terms, this meant that for every bid, OVL had to go to the CCEA for approval. The whole process could take up to 6 months – which wouldn't work if you are trying to close a transaction quickly.

In 2002–2003, oil prices started moving up and peak-oil was a real fear at the time. It took almost a decade – with shale oil in the US becoming commercially viable, for those fears to dissipate. The fear that oil may no longer be easily available gave impetus to India's quest for global energy assets.

ONGC Videsh

ONGC Videsh was set up as a 100% subsidiary of ONGC set up to acquire exploration blocks and discovered fields outside India. While the company was set up in the 1960s, it was dormant for a long time. In the early 1990s, OVL had stake in one block in Vietnam, where natural gas was discovered. Surprisingly, the board of the company and the petroleum ministry at the time felt that it would be difficult to manage an overseas asset, even though OVL was not the operator. OVL's then management had to convince the parent and the ministry both, to not sell the asset.

The first major acquisition by OVL was in 2001, a 20% stake in Sakhalin-1 – an offshore oil project on Russia's Pacific coast, near the Sakhalin Island. Oil had been discovered in Sakhalin much earlier, but development started after the fall of the Soviet Union – partly because technologies to develop the field were not available with the USSR. This project had three partners: ExxonMobil (30%, Operator), SODECO (30%) – a consortium of Japanese companies and Rosneft (40%). Rosneft was facing a cash crunch at the time and approached ONGC to sell a part of its stake. Rosneft wanted ONGC to pay its full share of future development costs as a part of the deal. Sakhalin-1 has proven to be among the most profitable of ONGC's acquisitions.

In 2001, ONGC also got a new Chairman & Managing Director – Subir Raha, one of the most dynamic public sector executives in India. Raha drove the acquisition of MRPL, a loss-making petroleum refinery, which was subsequently turned around – an investment that yielded over 1,000% returns to ONGC since. Raha's tenure coincides with OVL's acquisitions picking up steam. In 2002, OVL acquired a 25% stake in an oil field in Sudan, the Greater Nile Oil Project. This stake was being sold by Talisman Energy, a Canadian company. This was before Sudan was split into two countries (Sudan and South-Sudan), and the Arab government of Sudan was accused of perpetrating human rights violations on Christian minority – making it difficult for a Western company to operate in that country. Talisman faced demonstrations in Canada from human rights groups and decided to exit Sudan, selling its stake to ONGC. The due diligence for the Sudan deal had been conducted assuming the oil price at $18/barrel, a very conservative number. As a result, while the asset ran into troubles later – with the civil war in Sudan, ONGC was able to recover its investment and make a profit on it as well.

As OVL was gaining momentum, oil prices began to rise after a long time, and the government decided to go for equity oil overseas. In the case of OVL, the company – ONGC, acted first, with the government/policy following later.

Over the years, OVL acquired properties in West Asia, Africa and South America.

In 2013, OVL was close to acquiring an 8.4% stake in Kashagan – a massive oil field in Kazakhstan, for $5 billion. China's CNPC, with the support of the Chinese government, stole the deal from under OVL. This was a common occurrence at the time. Luckily for OVL, the stolen deals meant it didn't end up buying assets at the peak of the market. In 2016, after oil prices crashed, OVL had a major success – it acquired a 26% stake (with three other Indian companies buying another 23.9%) in Vankorneft, a major Russian oil field that produces 324,000 barrels/day (16 million tons/year) of oil. Such a deal would have been unimaginable 10-years back – the price would have been unaffordable. OVL is now India's second largest oil company, with annual oil and equivalent production of 15 million tons, with assets spread across over two dozen countries.

Not every venture has been successful – a case in point is Venezuela. In 2010, OVL, IOC and Oil India took up a combined 18% stake in the consortium to develop a project in the Orinoco Heavy Oil Belt. This was a government-to-government initiative – the Bolivarian Republic of Venezuela controls all aspects of the economy. Venezuela's national oil company, PDVSA, has a 60% stake in this project. This project aimed to produce 400,000 barrels/day of oil had seemed a coup at the time. However, the mismanaged Venezuelan economy has since run into a major self-inflicted crisis, exacerbated by American sanctions. Venezuela has seen a bout of hyperinflation, with its currency becoming worthless, and its oil production in 2019 was the lowest in 50 years. The production from this field in 2019 was 17,800 barrels/day, less than 5% of the target. OVL has another investment in Venezuela, a 40% stake in the San Cristobal project, with PDVSA as a 60% partner. While the project was making money, PDVSA couldn't pay out the dividends due to OVL, which ran up to over $500 million.

Money, not oil

Just after production started from Sakhalin-1, ONGC brought in a ship load of oil from Sakhalin to MRPL, its refinery in Mangalore. However, this physical movement of oil is more an exception than rule. Many of the investments made by OVL (and Bharat Petro Resources Limited, BPRL) are in remote locations with markets for that oil nearby. Shipping that oil to India will cost more than buying oil from closer sources. If the oil is not to be brought to India, then why invest in oil fields?

From 1947 to the present day, there hasn't been a single occasion when the physical flow of oil to India has been stopped. Given India's location – a week's sailing time from the world's largest oil suppliers, ships sailing to India have a relatively straightforward task. India's problems with oil have always been about money – how to pay for the oil. Thus, the investment in a foreign oil field is not for the physical possession of that particular volume of oil, but for the financial hedge that it provides. If the price of oil spikes up, so will the returns from selling oil from this asset, providing some protection against higher prices.

Competition with Chinese oil majors

As ONGC Videsh started scouting for oil fields, it ran into competition from China. China's state-owned oil companies, CNPC, Sinopec and CNOOC were on the same quest – to acquire overseas energy assets. They had a head start of nearly a decade and a much larger size. China currently produces 3.8 million barrels/day of oil domestically – it is the seventh largest oil producer globally and used to produce more oil than it consumed till the 1990s. During the 1990s, the strong economic growth outpaced local production and China turned a net importer of oil. Chinese companies started acquiring overseas oil assets at around the same time.

Because they served a much larger market, Chinese oil companies were much larger than their Indian counterparts. Oil production is the most profitable part of the petroleum supply chain, and China's upstream sector is about 4× of India's – giving the Chinese companies much larger balance sheets. Interviews with Indian oil industry executives at the time also indicated that the Chinese companies were often much more aggressive in bidding for these assets, and often had the explicit backing of the Chinese government – which would often weigh in with other offers to sweeten the deal.

An early example of this was in 2002, when OVL was negotiating with Japan's Japex for the latter's stake in a small Omani oil field, known as Block 5. The block was subsequently sold to China's CNPC for a significantly higher sum, as per reports at that time. However, the Chinese companies did not restrict themselves to outbidding India – sometimes they would 'steal' deals from under their Indian counterparts. A good example is the sale of Block-18 oil field in Angola – where Shell, which had a 50% stake, agreed to sell this to OVL.[12] Shell, the seller and OVL, the buyer, had agreed to the transaction. Almost at the last minute, China's Sinopec came in. The Chinese government made an offer the Angolan government could not refuse – an economic package worth $2 billion for various projects. In return, the Angolan government oil company, Sonangol, exercised its pre-emption rights to the oil field and acquired it. Sonangol subsequently brought in Sinopec as a partner in this oil field.[13]

Kashagan: cash all gone

The pinnacle of this approach was seen in the Kashagan deal. Kashagan is the largest of a group of four oil fields located in shallow waters, offshore Caspian Sea. With an estimated 9–13 billion barrels of recoverable oil, it is one of the largest oil discoveries in the past 40 years.[14] The local climate is extreme, and hostile, with winter temperatures of –30°C and summer peaks of 40°C. The shallow waters (3–4 m depth) in which the field is located freeze over in the winter – in all, making this an extremely challenging project.

The development of this field was eventually taken up by a consortium of global oil majors – Eni (operator), Total, Shell, ExxonMobil, KazMuniGaz (Kazakh NOC) and ConocoPhillips – a truly multinational undertaking with companies from Italy, France and the US. In 2013, OVL was in negotiation with ConocoPhillips, to purchase latter's 8.4% stake in the project, for $5 billion. This would have been the biggest overseas acquisition of ONGC to date. But at the last minute, the deal fell through. KazMuniGaz, the Kazakh NOC, exercised its pre-emption right to acquire the 8.4% stake on behalf of ConocoPhillips.[15] Almost simultaneously, it was reported that China's state-owned CNPC will acquire an 8.33% stake in the Kashagan project.[16]

The agreement was formalised during President Xi Jinping's visit to Kazakhstan in September 2013 – when the two countries inked a total of 22 agreements worth $30 billion.[17] Like in Angola, it is the additional incentives that China offered which swung the deal in its favour.

CNPC did ONGC a favour, though it didn't look like that at the time. The project ran into a mix of cost and time overruns and technical problems. Work on the project had started in 2005, with first oil production expected by 2010. Production finally started in September 2013 after multiple delays and then had to be stopped almost immediately.[18] The natural gas produced in Kashagan was rich in hydrogen sulphide, which corroded the pipelines used to bring the gas onshore. Production had to be stopped for almost 2 years, leading to further cost overruns.[19] The project earned the unfortunate moniker of 'Cash All Gone'.[20] CNN Money has rated Kashagan as the most expensive energy project of all time, at an estimated cost of $116 billion.[21]

Commercial production from Kashagan finally started in November 2016. However, over this period, the oil market had undergone a sea change. Increasing volumes of shale oil from the US brought down the price of oil from over $100/barrel in 2014 to under $50/barrel in 2016. CNPC ended up buying into Kashagan at the peak of the market, just before prices went into a long-term decline due to increasing oil supply. This was equally true for many other large energy assets acquired by Chinese companies in this period. The aggressive Chinese tactics saved ONGC from buying lemons. Then suddenly, Chinese energy acquisitions ground to a halt.

China's oil paralysis

China's state-owned oil companies, which were extremely active between 2002 and 2013, acquiring foreign oil fields, went really quiet from 2014 onwards. The drop in M&A activity happened even though oil prices had crashed, and assets were available at a much lower price than earlier. The reason for this is a mix of internal politics and weakening financials, the latter driven by the acquisition binge of the past decade.

This impasse that Chinese firms went through also shows the downside of a system where the dominant political party is closely intertwined with all sectors of the economy: most senior officials of state-owned companies are also members of the Chinese Communist Party.

Table 2.1 Top Chinese Energy Acquisitions of 2013

Acquiring Company	Acquisition Target	Stake Purchased	Value ($ bn)
CNOOC	Nexen (Canada)	100%	15.1
CNPC	Kashagan (Kazakhstan)	8.33%	5
CNPC	Area 4 (Mozambique)	20%	4.2

Source: International Energy Agency.

From 2002 to 2010, China's state-owned oil companies–led by Sinopec, CNOOC and PetroChina–spent $83.2 billion, acquiring oil and gas fields across the world, according to data compiled by the IEA. For the next three years (2011–2013), Chinese firms were in overdrive, spending an additional $72.5 billion on oil fields, IEA data shows. The year 2013 saw three of the biggest deals ever by Chinese firms (refer Table 2.1).

Chinese companies accounted for 35% of all petroleum deals greater than $1 billion during the year.[22]

Post 2013, however, acquisitions by Chinese companies fell off a cliff. During 2014, deal volume from China in the petroleum sector fell over 75%,[23] while during 2015, Chinese firms accounted for less than 1% of all acquisitions upstream.[24]

What changed?

The reason for this slowdown has been largely political. In December 2014, Zhou Yongkang, the former head of China's security services and a member of the 17th Politburo Standing Committee, was expelled from the Communist Party and arrested. In June 2015, he was sentenced to life in prison for corruption, and an estimated $14 billion worth of assets were seized from him and his family.[25] Zhou's sentencing had less to do with corruption and more to do with President Xi Jinping securing his own position – Zhou was a rival to President Xi.[26] His downfall is linked to the Chinese President Xi Jinping's drive to purge rivals from positions of influence.

A number of Zhou's supporters/protégés were also been stripped of their positions and sentenced to long prison terms.

Unfortunately for China's oil giants, Zhou's base of influence included the petroleum industry. He is a geophysical engineer and had worked in China's petroleum sector for 32 years and went on to head the China National Petroleum Corporation, the state-owned oil giant. Many of his supporters who were investigated and sentenced were also senior officials in the petroleum sector. The deals that they concluded,

Table 2.2 January–June Performance of China's State Oil Companies

	H1 2016	*H1 2015*
CNOOC[27]	–1.16	2.2
PetroChina[28]	0.079	3.80
Sinopec[29]	2.88	3.66
Figures in $ billion.		

including overseas acquisitions, were scrutinised for corruption.[30] Some of the biggest acquisitions, such as Nexen and Kashagan,[31] also ran into trouble.

The Chinese oil industry fell into the doldrums as far as external investments were concerned.

The fall in oil prices from 2014 to 2016 also did not help. Chinese companies bought most of their assets when the oil price was high and started losing money on these fields as oil price fell. Profitability dipped (refer Table 2.2). The reduced cash flows and their pre-existing capital expenditure commitments limited Chinese ability to buy new assets.

Pushback to Chinese investments

In 2005, CNOOC, one of the Chinese state-owned oil companies, placed a $18.5 billion bid to acquire Unocal, a leading US independent oil company. CNOOC gave three reasons for the acquisition. First, it would double CNOOC's existing production and increase its reserve base by 80%. Second, Unocal had most of its reserves and production in Asia, as did CNOOC – the combined entity would have 85% of its reserves in the world's fastest growing region. Third, the acquisition of gas-rich Unocal would give CNOOC a better balance between oil and natural gas.[32] However, the deal raised a political storm in the US. The acquisition of a large US enterprise by a state-owned Chinese company using subsidised funding from its parent government did not go down very well in a free-market America. There was also the issue of the potential impact on US energy security if a major American company were acquired by the Chinese government.[33] The US House of Representatives passed a resolution describing the deal as a threat to US energy security.[34] Public opinion was also hostile.[35] In face of the backlash, CNOOC withdrew from the deal.[36] Unocal was eventually acquired by Chevron, another American oil company.[37]

A somewhat similar chain of events happened to the north a few years later. In 2012, CNOOC bid for Nexen, a Canadian oil company operating in Alberta's oil sands. At almost the same time, Malaysia's state-owned Petronas bid for another company – Progress Energy. The Canadian government approved both the acquisitions but also indicated that more such deals will not be welcome. "When we say that Canada is open for business, we do not mean that Canada is for sale to foreign governments," Canadian Prime Minister Stephen Harper said at the time, describing these transactions as "end of a trend".[38] The state ownership of both the acquirers clearly played a role in the Canadian government's stand. CNOOC completed the acquisition in 2013.[39]

Both these countries now have additional guidelines in place to deal with takeovers of companies or assets by foreign government-owned companies. The Investment Canada Act, 1985,[40] governs such transactions in Canada while in the US, the Regulations pertaining to Mergers, Acquisitions, and Takeovers by Foreign Persons[41] govern such transactions. Such transactions are subject to a review to assess the benefits to the country as well as political influence in the transaction and any potential national security risks that may come up.[42,43] While China is still deeply invested in countries such as Angola, Kazakhstan and Venezuela, its model of state-backed capitalism is running into opposition in the developed world. These actions mirror the increasing opposition to China's One Belt, One Road initiative – now called a more benign Belt and Road Initiative.

BPRL

The other notable success story in India's quest for overseas oil has been BPRL – a fully owned subsidiary of public sector refiner Bharat Petroleum (BPCL). BPCL was the erstwhile Burmah Shell, a British-owned oil refiner and retailer, nationalised in 1976. By early 2000s, BPCL had a market share of one-quarter in the Indian oil market. It also owned three oil refineries – in Mumbai, Kochi and Numaligarh (as an independent company). At this time, the company was also in serious financial trouble, not of its own making.

During the 1990s, the Indian oil market operated under the administered price mechanism. The government set the prices of fuels such that companies could get a 'fair' return on their capital. In April 2002, APM was dismantled – for diesel and petrol, the key products. The retail companies – BPCL, HPCL and IOC, were free to revise retail selling price every month based on international trends. However, the free pricing system soon broke down, as petroleum prices started going up. A few months ahead of the 2004 general election, the BJP government quietly stopped the monthly price revisions (mostly upward).

The Congress-led UPA government which came in also didn't restore the monthly price revisions, even as petroleum price kept inching up.

Eventually, the three oil refiners – BPCL, HPCL and IOC – started losing money on diesel and petrol retail sales. The more they sold, the more they lost. An ugly word – 'underrecovery' – crept into the oil lexicon. Underrecovery was the difference between what the price of fuels should have been and what it was. These underrecoveries pushed the companies into losses. In 2007, petroleum prices touched an all-time high of $147/barrel. For the first six months of the financial year 2007–2008, the three public sector oil majors incurred Rs 26,362 crore![44] The government made up for these losses through a complex structure of cross-subsidies (from ONGC, Oil India and Gail) and by issuing oil-bonds in lieu of cash losses.

BPCL's losses were due to the high price of oil, a factor over which it had no control. The company's upstream venture was a way – very long term – of reducing this vulnerability. BPRL was incorporated in 2006 to implement BPCL's plans in oil exploration and production. Unlike ONGC, which was in the high margin business of oil exploration, BPCL was in the (then) lower margin business of oil refining and retail – it could not match ONGC and acquire known oil reserves. All it could afford to invest in at this point was exploratory acreage, which is cheaper. However, BPRL didn't have any expertise in oil exploration either, so it couldn't conduct the exploration on this acreage. Instead, BPRL sought out partners – Indian appliance maker Videocon was the first. The two companies jointly invested in a number of exploratory oil blocks including East Timor, Brazil and Mozambique. The operator in each of these blocks was another company, with an expertise in E&P. In the case of the Brazilian blocks, it was Petrobras, while in Mozambique, it was US oil independent Anadarko.

In 2008, the BPRL-Videocon consortium announced a discovery in Brazil. Later on, in 2010, Anadarko struck gas in offshore Mozambique. Rovuma Basin, where the discovery took place, has been one of the biggest gas discoveries worldwide in the past 20 years, with over 75 trillion cubic feet (equivalent to 12.5 billion barrels of oil) of natural gas reserves.

Alternative energy: tomorrow's fuels

Oil is not the only fuel driving the global economy, though it is the most visible, important and valuable. It is less abundant than coal – with a reserve/production ratio of 50 years, versus 132 years for coal. It is also less widely dispersed with much of the reserves located in

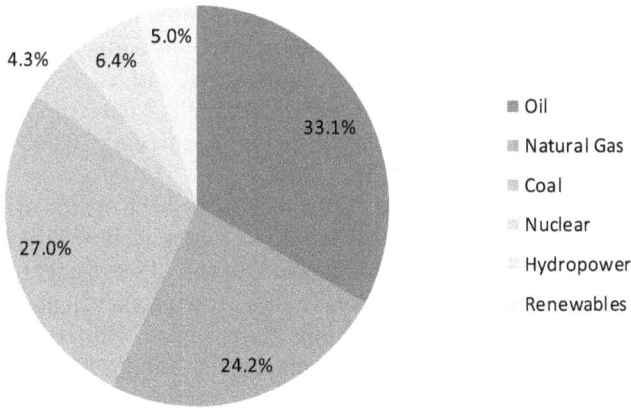

Figure 2.1 Global Energy Mix (2018)
Source: BP Statistical Review of World Energy, 2019

geopolitically unstable countries/regions. Fears of oil running out are almost as old as the oil age, and so has been the search for alternatives to oil. Two of the perennial favourites are atomic power and biofuels. There are tempting arguments for both.

Atomic energy: ever promising

Before the 1973 oil shock, almost a quarter of the world's electricity supply was produced by burning oil.[45] The high price of oil following the oil shocks put paid to burning oil in power plants. As oil lost ground, nuclear power took up some of that space. At the time, it was felt that nuclear power can be source of limitless energy, too cheap to be metered. That didn't happen. However, nuclear power has had a second lease of life in the new millennium as a source of 'clean' energy – unlike coal, generation of nuclear power doesn't release carbon dioxide into the atmosphere and doesn't cause global warming. The 2011 Fukushima disaster has also put paid to such hopes.

India has been an early adopter of nuclear power, with the two units of Tarapur Atomic Power Station starting commercial operations in 1969. However, India's ambitions to generate atomic power were set back by severe international sanctions following the 1974 Pokhran test. The Nuclear Suppliers Group – a group of countries that controls the trade and access to nuclear materials, equipment and technology – was set up in response to the Pokhran test.

From this point onward, India's ambitions to generate 'cheap' nuclear power were hobbled by a lack of fuel – India lacks sufficient domestic reserves of uranium, and imports were no longer possible. By 2001, India's nuclear power generation capacity added to 2,720 MW, accounting for less than 4% of India's total electricity supply. However, India had a very ambitious target – of achieving 20,000 MW of atomic power capacity by 2020.

The 2005 India–US nuclear agreement promised to speed up India's atomic power programme. This initiative, announced in July 2005 by Indian Prime Minister Manmohan Singh and US President George Bush, provided a process to meet India's growing energy needs while strengthening the global non-proliferation regime. Under this initiative, while India continued to remain outside the NPT, it agreed to separate its civil and military nuclear programmes and bring the civilian part of its nuclear programme under IAEA safeguards.[46] The Nuclear Suppliers Group granted *"an exception to its full-scope safeguards requirement to permit civil nuclear supply to India"* – meaning India could acquire nuclear technology and atomic fuels without formally joining NPT.

Commerce was one of the many drivers of the 123 agreement. India was and is one of the fastest growing global economies with an ever increasing energy demand. Meeting this demand would require energy from all sources, including atomic power. Russian and Western companies were expecting projects worth billions of dollars from India, to build new atomic power plants. India already had an agreement with Russia's Rosatom to build nuclear reactors in Kudankulam. It signed further agreements with three Western firms – GE and Westinghouse of the US and Areva of France, to build three additional atomic power plants. While the construction of the Kudankulam reactor had already started in 2000, the other reactors were at the MoU stage. One of the sticking points – why work on these reactors did not start, was the tricky clause on nuclear liability – what happens in case of an accident. The Fukushima disaster showed that there was virtually no upper limit to the financial damages from a nuclear accident, and India has bitter memory of the 1984 Bhopal gas disaster, where the US firm Union Carbide walked away with a slap on its wrist. Western companies were unwilling to take on the unlimited liability that could arise from an accident, while India was unwilling to let go. Eventually, technology resolved an issue that negotiators were unable to.

Finished by high costs

In November 2015, US-based renewable energy company SunEdison won a bid to sell solar power to India at a then record low price of Rs 4.63/unit. It wasn't an isolated bid – nine other companies had offer to sell electricity for less than Rs 5/unit at the time. Since then, costs of renewable energy have fallen to under Rs 4/unit. The closest comparison of nuclear power at that time was to the under-construction reactors at Kudankulam – Units 3 and 4, each of 1,000 MW. The projected cost of electricity from these units, if they were completed at cost, on time, was projected at Rs 6.3/unit in 2015. At that time, it was estimated that these two units will be completed by 2020–2021.

Of the various reactors that India wants to build with foreign collaboration, the Russian reactors are the cheapest. The cost of these units works out to $2.6 million/MW at 2020 exchange rates. The cost per megawatt of a Westinghouse reactor (in the US) worked out to an eye-popping $7 million/MW.[47] At these prices, the cost of nuclear power from Western-designed reactors is likely to be well over Rs 10/unit. The capital outlay for a thermal (coal) or renewable power plant is less than $1 million/MW, while NTPC, India's largest coal power producer, supplied electricity at Rs 3.38/unit during FY19. The high upfront costs of nuclear power compared to alternatives – coal and renewable – make it financially unviable.

The other problem with nuclear power is that rarely are projects completed at cost, on time. The first two units of the Kudankulam Atomic Power Plant are a case in point – work had started on these two units in 2000 and was supposed to be completed by 2008. The first of these units was finally commissioned in 2014. Units 3 and 4 of this plant were supposed to be finished by 2020–2021. By March 2019, the physical progress on these two was 28%. Another example, from the Western world, is the Olkiluoto 3 reactor in Finland, being built by Areva. Work on this reactor had started in 2005 and was supposed to be completed by 2009. The project has faced multiple delays and cost overruns and was still under construction in 2019, 12 years behind schedule.[48] The large size and the complexity of these projects mean inevitable delays, pushing up the already high costs.

The unresolved issue of nuclear liability and the high upfront costs mean that nuclear power will play a small role in India's energy profile, at least for the foreseeable future.

In this scenario, the only viable alternative for India is a third technology – the indigenously developed Pressurized Heavy Water Reactors (PHWR). Based on under-construction projects, this technology has a lower capital cost – of Rs 14.6 crore ($1.96 million)/MW – less than the Russian tech and only a fraction of the price of western designs. Since the reactors and equipment are being supplied by Indian suppliers, the issue of a foreign supplier escaping liability also doesn't arise.

The biggest benefit of the India–US nuclear agreement is not going to the atomic power plants, but the free availability of fuel, which will enable India to continue building indigenously designed, cost-effective reactors.

Biofuels: converting food into fuel

Biofuels are a tempting idea, on the surface. Why not 'grow' our own fuel instead of paying billions of dollars to the Arabs? However, this simplistic question reduces everything to domestic versus foreign, without factoring issues such as costs, use of capital and second- and third-order effects.

The latest biofuel craze took off globally in the 2003–2007 period, when oil prices touched all-time highs, crossing the $100 per barrel mark. Brazil, which has abundant availability of fertile land and water, has long been a producer of biofuels – ethanol from sugarcane. Other countries tried to follow this model in the 2003–2007 period, the US and EU among them. Both provided subsidies to farmers for growing biofuels – corn/maize in the US and rapeseed in the EU. In 2006, the Food and Agricultural Organization (FAO, a UN body) Food Price Index went up by 7.7%, followed by a 26% increase in 2007 and another 25% in 2008. Food prices, measured by this index, were almost 70% higher than the levels in 2005.[49] While a range of factors contributed to this, biofuels also played a role. In 2007, 12% of the global maize output (mostly in the US) and 25% of the global rapeseed oil output (almost entirely in the EU) was diverted to biofuels.[50] This impacted food prices because:

1   Diversion of these food products to biofuels automatically pushes up their price.
2   If these products become more financially lucrative (because of subsidies), then farmers in food-exporting countries will divert land to these at the expense of other crops such as wheat, pushing up prices of other food products as well.

Fidel Castro had slammed biofuels as a 'sinister plot to convert food into fuel'.[51] He was proven right. There are some additional issues with biofuels. First, the cultivation of any agricultural crop requires the use of fertilisers – some of which are derived from petroleum. Agriculture in the rich world, which is highly mechanised, uses up a lot of fuel as well. Taking these into account, the net fuel produced by cultivating biofuels is much less than what the production figures suggest. Biofuels seem to be more about providing income support to rich world farmers than replacing fossil fuels.

As an agricultural, oil-deficient country, 'growing our own oil' has proven to be one idea almost impossible to put debunk in India. Luckily, no large-scale diversion of agricultural land to biofuels has taken place in India. However, it has tried home-grown alternatives.

In 2003, India came out with its first biofuel policy. At that time, two major institutions – Indian Railways and Indian Oil – also experimented with biodiesel cultivation. Biodiesel was to be produced from the seeds of the Jatropha plant – which were to be cultivated on barren land and along railway tracks. Barren/fallow land was to be used as it was felt that using fertile agricultural land would affect food production/prices and availability. Two of India's public sector oil majors – IOC and BPCL – formed joint ventures for the large-scale production of biodiesel. Both eventually had to be wound up due to operational and financial problems. Barren land, by definition, is not capable of supporting plants. If it can't support other plants, the likelihood that it will offer rich yields of biodiesel is low. Without irrigation and fertilisers, expecting large yields of biodiesel year after year from the same land is also not realistic. The biodiesel idea has been junked, but the underlying concept still remains.

India has a policy for blending ethanol (produced from molasses – leftovers after producing sugar), with petrol. The declared policy is to have an ethanol blend of 20% in all the petrol sold within the country,[52] in practice, a blend of 5% has been achieved[53] – more ethanol is just not available. During FY20, petrol accounted for 14% of India's oil consumption – 5% of that works out to 0.7% of India's total oil consumption – not enough to make a difference. The big benefit of ethanol blending is to provide income support for sugarcane farmers, not substitution of imported oil. On the cost front, sugarcane is grown on 4.91 million hectares of fertile agricultural land[54] and is held responsible for the depletion of the groundwater table in several agricultural regions.

Notes

1 Ministry of Petroleum and Natural Gas, Government of India. 2000. "Annual Report 1999–2000." New Delhi.
2 Petroleum Planning & Analysis Cell. 2020. "PPAC's Snapshot of India's Oil and Gas Data." New Delhi: PPAC, Ministry of Petroleum and Natural Gas.
3 Office of the Historian. 2018. "Milestones: 1969–1976 – Office of the Historian." State.gov. 2018. https://history.state.gov/milestones/1969-1976/oil-embargo
4 Ministry of Finance Government of India. 1974. "Economic Survey 1974–75." https://www.indiabudget.gov.in/budget_archive/es1974-75%202/1%20 The%20Economy%20in%201974-75.pdf
5 Ministry of Finance Government of India. 1974. "Economic Survey 1974–75." https://www.indiabudget.gov.in/budget_archive/es1974-75%202/1%20 The%20Economy%20in%201974-75.pdf
6 Ministry of Finance Government of India. 1980. "Economic Survey 1979–80." https://www.indiabudget.gov.in/budget_archive/es1979-80/1%20The %20Economic%20Situation%20in%201979-80.pdf
7 Graefe, Laurel. 2013. "Oil Shock of 1978–79 | Federal Reserve History." Federalreservehistory.org. 2013. https://www.federalreservehistory.org/essays/oil_shock_of_1978_79.
8 Ministry of Finance Government of India. 1982. "Economic Survey 1981–82." https://www.indiabudget.gov.in/budget_archive/es1981-82/1%20Economic %20situation%20in%201981-82.pdf
9 Office of the Historian. 2019. "Milestones: 1989–1992." State.gov. 2019. https://history.state.gov/milestones/1989-1992/gulf-war
10 Ministry of Finance Government of India. 1992. "Economic Survey 1991–92." https://www.indiabudget.gov.in/budget_archive/es1991-92_A/2%20 The%20Payments%20Crisis.pdf
11 Cairn Energy. n.d. "Cairn | Investment in India." www.cairnenergy.com. https://www.cairnenergy.com/investors/investment-in-india/
12 Rigzone. 2004. "ONGC Videsh to Acquire 50% Stake in Block 18 Offshore Angola." www.rigzone.com. 2004. https://www.rigzone.com/news/oil_gas/a/12230/ongc_videsh_to_acquire_50_stake_in_block_18_offshore_angola/
13 Financial Express. 2005. "Angola Snubs Indias Oil Advances." *The Financial Express*, March 8, 2005. https://www.financialexpress.com/archive/angola-snubs-indias-oil-advances/128824
14 North Caspian Operating Company. n.d. "NCOC about North Caspian Project." www.ncoc.kz. https://www.ncoc.kz/en/ncoc/about
15 ONGC India. 2013. "Republic of Kazakhstan pre-empts ONGC Videsh bid to acquire ConocoPhillips stake in North Caspian Sea Production Sharing Agreement (NCS PSA) that includes Kazakhstan's Kashagan field." https://www.ongcindia.com/wps/wcm/connect/en/media/press-release/republic-of-kazakhstan-pre-empts-ongc-videsh-bid-to-acquire-conocophillips-stake-in-north-caspian-sea-production-sharing-agreement-ncs-psa-that-includes-kazakhstan-s-kashagan-fiel
16 Modi, Ajay. 2013. "India Loses Giant Kashagan Oil Field to China." *India Today*, 2013. https://www.indiatoday.in/business/story/india-loses-giant-kashagan-oil-field-to-china-168906-2013-07-02

17 Gordeyeva, Mariya. 2013. "China Buys into Giant Kazakh Oilfield for $5 Billion." *Reuters*, September 7, 2013. https://www.reuters.com/article/us-oil-kashagan-china/china-buys-into-giant-kazakh-oilfield-for-5-billion-idUSBRE98606620130907
18 Crude Accountability. 2017. "The Kashgan Oil Bubble." https://crudeac countability.org/wp-content/uploads/ENG_Kashagan_report_Final1-1.pdf
19 Vukmanovic, Oleg, and Stephen Jewkes. 2014. "Kashagan Oil Field: Stuck between 'a Widow Maker' and 'a Rotating Bomb.'" *Reuters*, April 2, 2014. https://www.reuters.com/article/us-oil-kashagan-insight/kashagan-oil-field-stuck-between-a-widow-maker-and-a-rotating-bomb-idUSBRE A310WE20140402
20 Chazan, Guy. 2007. "In Caspian, Big Oil Fights Ice, Lethal Fumes – and Kazakhs." *Wall Street Journal*, August 28, 2007, sec. News. https://www.wsj.com/articles/SB118824035440810037
21 Hargreaves, Steve. 2012. "World's 10 Most Expensive Energy Projects." *CNNMoney*, August 27, 2012. https://money.cnn.com/gallery/news/econ-omy/2012/08/27/expensive-energy-projects/10.html
22 EY. 2013. "Global Oil and Gas Transactions Review 2013." Ernst & Young.
23 EY. 2014. "Global Oil and Gas Transactions Review 2014." Ernst & Young.
24 EY. 2015. "Global Oil and Gas Transactions Review 2015." Ernst & Young.
25 Wu, Yuwen. 2015. "Profile: China's Fallen Security Chief Zhou Yong-kang." *BBC News*, October 12, 2015, sec. China. http://www.bbc.com/news/world-asia-china-26349305
26 Chinascope. 2016. "Political Rivalry in China Part 1 – Plots to Overthrow Xi Jinping-Chinascope." Chinascope.org, 2016. http://chinascope.org/archives/7861?doing_wp_cron=1591241743.4678699970245361328125
27 CNOOC Limited. 2016. "Announcement of 2016 Interim Results." https://www1.hkexnews.hk/listedco/listconews/sehk/2016/0824/ltn20160824233.pdf
28 PetroChina Company Limited. 2016. "Announcement of the Interim Results for the Six Months ended June 30, 2016." https://www1.hkexnews.hk/listedco/listconews/sehk/2016/0824/ltn20160824235.pdf
29 China Petroleum & Chemical Corporation. 2016. "Interim Results An-nouncement For The Six Months Ended 30 June 2016." https://www1.hkexnews.hk/listedco/listconews/sehk/2016/0828/ltn20160828139.pdf
30 Zhu, Charlie, David Lague, and Benjamin Kang Lim. 2014. "Inside the Purge of China's Oil Mandarins." Thomson Reuters.
31 Zhdannikov, Dmitry. 2014. "Megaprojects a Megaheadache for Oil Bosses." *Reuters*, January 22, 2014. https://uk.reuters.com/article/us-davos-oil-megaprojects-idUSBREA0L1EV20140122
32 CNOOC Limited. 2005. "CNOOC Limited Proposes Merger with Un-ocal Offering US$67 per Share in Cash." https://www.cnoocltd.com/art/2005/6/23/art_8431_1130421.html
33 Expressing The Sense Of The House That A Chinese State-Owned En-ergy Company Could Take Action That Would Threaten The United States." *Congressional Record.* 151: 90 (June 30 2005). https://www.congress.gov/congressional-record/2005/06/30/house-section/article/H5570-2
34 VOA News. 2009. "Chinese Bid for UNOCAL Sparks Sharp De-bate in US Congress | Voice of America – English." www.voanews.

com. 2009. https://www.voanews.com/archive/chinese-bid-unocal-sparks-sharp-debate-us-congress

35 VOA News. 2009. "American Public Hostile to Chinese Bid for Unocal | Voice of America – English." www.voanews.com. 2009. https://www.voanews.com/archive/american-public-hostile-chinese-bid-unocal

36 CNOOC Limited. 2005. "CNOOC Limited to Withdraw Unocal Bid." https://www.cnoocltd.com/art/2005/8/2/art_8431_1130461.html

37 ChevronTexaco Corp. 2005. "ChevronTexaco Announces Agreement to Acquire Unocal." https://chevroncorp.gcs-web.com/news-releases/news-release-details/chevrontexaco-announces-agreement-acquire-unocal

38 Puzic, Sonja. 2012. "Ottawa Approves $15B Chinese Takeover of Nexen." *CTVNews*, December 7, 2012. https://www.ctvnews.ca/canada/ottawa-approves-15b-chinese-takeover-of-nexen-1.1070698

39 CNOOC Limited. 2013. "CNOOC Limited Completes Acquisition of Nexon Inc." https://www.cnoocltd.com/art/2013/2/26/art_8351_1663741.html

40 Investment Canada Act, 1985. c. 28. http://laws.justice.gc.ca/eng/F-5.5/index.htm

41 Department of Treasury. "Regulations Pertaining to Mergers, Acquisitions, and Takeovers by Foreign Persons." *Federal Register* 73, no. 226 (November 21, 2008) https://www.treasury.gov/resource-center/international/foreign-investment/Documents/CFIUS-Final-Regulations-new.pdf

42 Defense Production Act of 1950. S 721. https://www.treasury.gov/resource-center/international/foreign-investment/Documents/Section-721-Amend.pdf

43 Bhandari, Amit, and Kunal Kulkarni. 2016. "North America: Petro State." *Gateway House*, April 13, 2016. https://www.gatewayhouse.in/petro-state/

44 Ministry of Petroleum and Natural Gas, Government of India. "Losses to Oil Companies." Lok Sabha. Question no 12. 2007. loksabhaph.nic.in/Questions/QResult15.aspx?qref=54270&lsno=14

45 International Atomic Energy Agency. 1990. "World Electricity Generation, Nuclear Power, and Oil Markets." IAEA.

46 Bureau of Public Affairs, Department Of State. The Office of Electronic Information. 2008. "U.S.-India Civil Nuclear Cooperation Initiative." 2001–2009. State.gov. October 15, 2008. https://2001-2009.state.gov/p/sca/rls/fs/2008/109567.htm

47 Taxpayers for Common Sense. 2014. "Vogtle Reactors 3&4 Fact Sheet." Taxpayers for Common Sense. February 19, 2014. http://www.taxpayer.net/energy-natural-resources/doe-loan-guarantee-program-vogtle-reactors-34/.

48 Yle. 2019. "Olkiluoto 3 Reactor Delayed yet Again, Now 12 Years behind Schedule." *YleUutiset*, December 20, 2019. https://yle.fi/uutiset/osasto/news/olkiluoto_3_reactor_delayed_yet_again_now_12_years_behind_schedule/11128489.

49 Food and Agriculture Organisation of the United Nations. 2013. "FAO Food Price Index | World Food Situation | Food and Agriculture Organization of the United Nations." Fao.org. 2013. http://www.fao.org/worldfoodsituation/foodpricesindex/en/

50 Food and Agriculture Organization of the United Nations. 2009. "The State of Agricultural Commodity Markets 2009." FAO. http://www.fao. org/3/i0854e/i0854e00.htm

51 The Guardian. 2007. "Castro Warns Poor Will Starve for Greener Fuel." *The Guardian*, March 29, 2007. https://www.theguardian.com/environment/ 2007/mar/29/energy.cuba.

52 Ministry of Petroleum and Natural Gas, Government of India. "Biofuel Policy, 2018." Lok Sabha. Question 407. 2020. http://164.100.24.220/ loksabhaquestions/annex/173/AS407.pdf

53 Petroleum Planning & Analysis Cell. 2020. "PPAC's Snapshot of India's Oil and Gas Data." New Delhi: PPAC, Ministry of Petroleum and Natural Gas.

54 Shukla, S. K., Lalan Sharma, S. K. Awasthi, and A. D. Pathak. 2017. "Sugarcane in India." Lucknow: ICAR – Indian Institute of Sugarcane Research.

3 Flashpoints and chokepoints

Oil is not just about commerce. From before World War I, when Royal Navy decided to shift to oil propulsion – triggering a worldwide search for oil – geopolitics has played a large role in the global oil trade. On top of that, there are domestic and regional complications of the oil-rich countries. Whether oil-rich countries – Iraq, Iran, Libya, Sudan and Venezuela – are more unstable or whether instability in oil-rich countries gets reported more is an academic argument. For India, the big concern is that this instability eventually leads to disruptions, which in turn lead to higher prices.

India needs to monitor multiple stress points and ever-present risks that can blow up, requiring monitoring and mitigation. Some of these are natural geographical choke points and others are long-simmering regional rivalries. One emerging issue for India is the rising economic heft of China and the security issues that it creates, particularly the China–Pakistan military nexus.

Sanctions

In ancient times, siegecraft used to be a big part of war – blocking food and other supplies to make a besieged city come to terms. In the modern era, it has become possible to separate the act of blockading from a shooting war – through sanctions. Sanctions are an economic act – blocking the flow of goods or money, to achieve a political outcome – regime change or a change in domestic/international policies of the target country.[1]

The US had imposed economic sanctions on Japan in 1940–1941, blocking Japanese funds in the US and stopping oil supplies to Japan to stop it from attacking China – which eventually culminated in the attack on Pearl Harbor and the Pacific war. In the post-WW2 era, sanctions have mostly been used by the US and its European allies – out of the 174 documented impositions of sanctions, the US

DOI: 10.4324/9781003152927-3

deployed sanctions on 109 occasions, followed by the UK (16), EU (14) and the former USSR (13).[2]

In the post-Cold War era, the sanctions that really matter are the ones imposed/supported by the US. These sanctions prohibit US entities (persons and companies) from dealings with proscribed entities (persons and companies) of the target country. American sanctions bite because of the central role played by the US dollar in international commerce – most of the global trade is conducted in the US dollar. Any dollar-denominated trade at some point will have to pass through the US banking system – which will refuse to conduct business with the proscribed entity. As a result, the sanctioned entity effectively loses access to international finance – it can no longer conduct international business. For any multinational corporation, this is a death sentence, and companies are willing to pay massive fines rather than run this risk. In 2014, French bank BNP Paribas agreed to pay $8.97 billion as settlement to US authorities for violating sanctions against Cuba, Iran and Sudan.[3] In 2018, another French bank, Societe Generale, agreed to pay penalties adding up to $1.8 billion for facilitating transactions involving Cuba and Iran.[4] HSBC agreed to pay $1.256 billion in 2012 for similar violations.[5]

Certain Indian entities, linked to India's nuclear and space programmes, have been sanctioned by the US in the past – after the 1998 atomic tests. Those days are long gone as the interests of India and the US converge. The present issue is the imposition of sanctions on India's trade and energy partners. From the Indian perspective, the sanctions that matter are those on Iran, Venezuela and Russia.

Iran has been under US sanctions more or less since the 1979 Islamic Revolution. The sanctions have progressively hardened as Iran has pursued nuclear weapons. In 2016, under then US President Obama, six countries (China, France, Germany, Russia, the UK and the US) and Iran concluded an agreement – the Joint Comprehensive Plan of Action, under which Iran agreed to roll back its atomic programme in return for significant relief on economic sanctions.[6] However, in late 2016, the US elected a new President – Donald Trump – who withdrew from the JCPOA, reimposing sanctions on Iran. All this matters because Iran has the world's fourth largest reserves of oil and second largest reserves of natural gas – almost one-sixth of the known global gas reserves. Historically, Iran has been among the top suppliers of oil to India. However, from $12 billion worth of oil imports in 2018–2019, oil imports from Iran fell by nearly 90% in 2019–2020 as the US reimposed sanctions on Iran. India's ONGC also had the rights to develop an Iranian gas field – Farzad B, in the Persian Gulf, a project which is unlikely to see the light of the day. Given the current reality, Iran is likely to remain locked out of the global energy market for the foreseeable future.

Russia is also under US sanctions, but not quite as wide ranging as those on Iran. Sanctions were imposed on Russia following its annexation of Crimea in 2014, and following allegations of meddling in US elections. The most stringent sanctions target Russian defence manufacturers – which affects India as it has been and remains a major buyer of Russian military hardware since the 1960s. Less stringent sanctions target Russia's energy sector. While India doesn't directly import oil from Russia, Indian companies are invested heavily in the Russian oil and gas sector. Sakhalin I, Imperial Energy and Vankorneft are among the largest energy investments made by Indian companies worldwide. Russia has been in the top-three oil producers and exporters for decades and is also the largest producer and exporter of natural gas. Sanctions on Russia are designed in a way that they don't affect Russia's existing oil and gas trade – such a disruption would severely damage the economies of American allies in Europe. The sanctions are designed to cut off future flows of Russian oil and gas – specific sanctions target exploration and development of Arctic and shale reserves of Russia.

Venezuela has the world's largest reserves of oil – over 300 billion barrels. But economic mismanagement under socialist policies of Hugo Chavez (1999–2013) and his successor Nicolas Maduro (2013 onward) has seen the country plunged into economic collapse. By 2020, Venezuela's oil production fell to a multi-decade low. Sanctions on Venezuela target individuals of the Maduro regime as well as state-owned oil company PDVSA, making it difficult to export oil.[7]

Sanctions on these countries may have a political justification; they also bring an economic benefit to the US. With the increasing production of shale gas, the US has become an exporter of liquefied natural gas. Russia and Iran together account for one-third of global natural gas reserves. Locking these two countries out of the market will improve the prospects (and prices) of the US-sourced natural gas.

The other point about sanctions is that they are easy to impose but very hard to withdraw. Iran has been under various sanctions for over four decades, and there is no sign of sanctions on Russia coming off. In this scenario, India will have to factor in the disruptive impact of sanctions in planning its energy security.

Saudi–Iran rivalry

Saudi Arabia and Iran, on the two sides of the Persian Gulf, are the largest countries in West Asia – in size, wealth and influence. They also represent two opposing world views. Saudi Arabia follows Sunni Islam, while Iran is Shia. Most of Saudi Arabia's oil is in its eastern province of Qatif, which has a Shia majority and is a potential hotspot for the Kingdom. Saudi Arabia is a monarchy, while Iran is an Islamic Republic that overthrew a monarchy. During the Iran–Iraq war that followed the Islamic Revolution, Saudi Arabia and its Gulf allies provided significant financial and military support to Iraq. The US, which guarantees the security of Saudi Arabia and other GCC monarchies and harbours a deep antipathy towards the Iranian regime, also gets drawn into these disputes.

In June 2017, Saudi Arabia and its allies [the UAE, Bahrain, Egypt, Maldives and Yemen (Saudi supported faction)] separately announced that they were cutting diplomatic ties with Qatar.[8] Reasons given were Qatar's support for Al Qaeda, Deash, the Muslim Brotherhood and other destabilising forces, and use of Qatar-based media (Al Jazeera) to fan unrest in other Arab/GCC countries.[9] Saudi Arabia prohibited overflights by Qatari aircraft, and Saudi officials even hinted at digging a canal at Saudi–Qatar border, bringing about a physical separation of the two countries.[10] All trade with Qatar, including food exports were prohibited. Iran stepped into the breach almost immediately – sending containers of fresh produce to Qatar almost immediately[11] sending over 1,000 tons per day of foodstuffs to the Emirate.[12] Unlike the other Gulf monarchies, Qatar had relatively close ties with Iran – this is because the two countries share South Pars – the world's largest gas field. Qatar has become the world's largest LNG exporter because of its share of the field, while Iran is unable to develop and sell LNG due to sanctions.

In the present day, the Saudi–Iran confrontation is playing out in Yemen, which is facing a disastrous civil war, with Saudi Arabia-led alliance supporting the government and Iran supporting the Houthi rebels. Saudi Arabia intervened in Yemen with boots on the ground in 2015 and was still embroiled in 2020. News reports from Yemen indicate that the war is not going well for Saudi Arabia, the Kingdom and its allies have taken heavy losses in men and material in Yemen. The Houthi militia has also been able to assemble simple ballistic rockets, which they have used to attack targets hundreds of kilometres inside Saudi Arabia, including Riyadh.

On 14 September 2019, an oil-processing plant in Abqaiq, Saudi Arabia, owned and operated by Saudi Aramco, was attacked by drones and missiles. These attacks resulted in a drop of 5.7 million barrels/day in Aramco's (and the world's) oil production. A disruption of this magnitude has never happened in the oil world before – this attack temporarily took more oil offline than the Iranian revolution of

1979. Because of well-supplied oil markets, this attack caused only a temporary and a relatively small blip in prices. During the early 2000s, the oil market was so tight that even news of terror attacks was enough to push up the prices more. Houthis claimed responsibility for this attack, but Saudi Arabia[13] and the US blamed Iran for it. Investigations also suggested that the direction of the attack and its sophistication ruled out Houthi participation and hinted at a more direct Iranian role instead.[14] A few months later, on 2 January 2020, in a drone strike, the US killed Qasem Soleimani – the head of Iran's Islamic Revolutionary Guards Corps-Quds Force, an organisation that is part of the Iranian regime and is blamed by the US for numerous terrorist actions.[15] In turn, Iran fired a number of missiles at an Iraqi military base that hosted US troops. Iran claimed it had inflicted severe casualties, and having satisfied the need for retaliation, it drew back. While this particular confrontation didn't escalate, there were fears for some time that it might.

These actions show that while Saudi Arabia (and the US) and Iran have not come down to a shooting war yet, there is enough action going on via proxies, and it could potentially escalate into a wider conflagration, which would impact oil production and exports in this region.

Straits of Hormuz

The reason Saudi–Iran rivalry matters is evident if we look at a map of the Persian Gulf region's oil fields. The oil fields of Saudi Arabia, Iran, Iraq, Kuwait, the UAE and Qatar – which together account for almost half of the world's known oil reserves and one-third of the current global oil production – are all located around the Persian Gulf. To reach their markets, this oil has to be loaded onto ships in the Persian Gulf and then sail through the Straits of Hormuz – a narrow channel 21 nautical miles wide at its narrowest – to reach consumers in Asia and elsewhere.

One of the big perennial concerns of the global oil trade is the risk of the Straits of Hormuz being shut for commerce by Iran. It is felt that any such move by the Iranian regime is likely to lead to a swift global response, possibly removing it. Therefore, the Iranian regime is likely to resort to such a step only if it feels an existential threat. Iran mined the straits in the 1980s, during the Iran–Iraq war – when the new regime was literally fighting for survival.

There was also a phase in the Iran–Iraq war known as the Tanker War, when air forces of Iran and Iraq started attacking oil tankers carrying oil exports of the other side. Hundreds of vessels were attacked

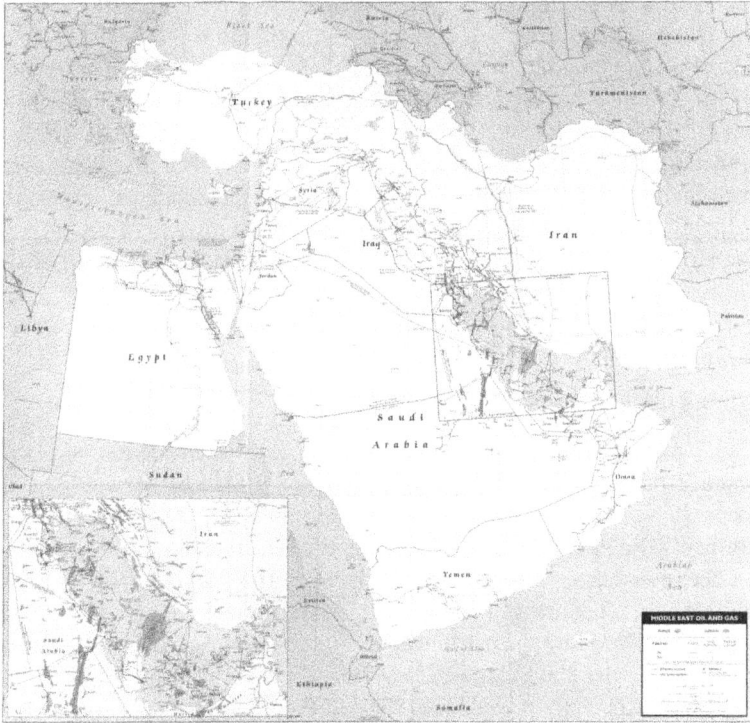

Figure 3.1 Map of Persian Gulf Oil Fields (Library of Congress, US)[16]

in this period. This disrupted oil exports to the rest of the world – and also pushed up insurance rates for shipping in the region. India, as a buyer of Iranian and Iraqi goods, was also affected. Indian flagged vessels of Shipping Corporation of India (public sector) and GE Shipping (private) used to do the Gulf-India run at that time. Vessels had to take extra precautions in that period – ships would depart from India at night, without informing anyone, including the owner, in order to keep their exact whereabouts secret. The SCI supertanker Kanchenjunga was attacked in December 1984 by Iranian aircraft while fully laden; thankfully there was no loss of life.

In 2019, there were attacks on oil tankers around the Straits of Hormuz, but nowhere on the scale of the Iran–Iraq war. Although Iran was blamed for these attacks, it denied responsibility.

The GCC countries recognise this vulnerability and have tried to mitigate it. Saudi Arabia has tried to reduce its vulnerability to the straits by piping some of its oil into the Red Sea and export-ing it via a new terminal, Yanbu.[17] This pipeline has a capacity of 3 million barrels/day, which is about 25% of the peak Saudi output. Saudi Arabia has another pipeline – the Iraqi Pipeline in Saudi Ara-bia (IPSA) – built in 1989 to carry Iraqi oil while bypassing the Per-sian Gulf. However, this pipeline stopped operating in 1990 – after Iraq invaded Kuwait. Abu Dhabi has also constructed the Habshan-Fujiriah pipeline, linking its oil fields with the Gulf of Oman bypass-ing Hormuz, which can ship 1.5 million barrels/day, about half of the UAE's exports.[18]

However, Iraq and Kuwait have no access other than the Red Sea.

Global choke points

The Strait of Hormuz matters because it is a maritime choke point. A maritime choke point is a natural point of congestion that a ship needs to pass – connecting two bigger water bodies. The Strait of Hormuz connects the Persian Gulf to the Arabian Sea. The biggest security for an ocean-going vessel is the vast expense of the ocean itself – it can be hidden in the vastness of the seas. A choke point takes away this pro-tection, making the ship vulnerable. The major maritime choke points in the world are the Straits of Hormuz, the Malacca Straits, the Suez Canal and the Bab al Mandab, the Panama Canal, the Straits of Gi-braltar and the Straits of Bosphorus.

World powers have tried to control these choke points. Suez Canal and Gibraltar were an important part of Britain's imperial strategy. The Panama Canal allowed the US navy to move its fleets between the Pacific and Atlantic Oceans – the US was the first country to recognise Panama's independence, protected Panama against Colombia and got a perpetual lease on the canal in return.

For India, the Strait of Hormuz is the one choke point that really matters – because it has an immediate impact on energy flows to India. The Malacca Straits matter to the East Asian economies – China, Ja-pan and South Korea – because of oil sailing from West Asia to East Asia has to use them. Because of this double vulnerability – Hormuz and Malacca and the long sailing times of over a month, the East Asian countries have had to invest heavily in building up strategic petroleum reserves, to guard against disruptions.

While not strictly choke points, two other geographical features also put India's energy flows at risk – the Pakistani Port of Gwadar and the Gulf of Kutch in India.

Gwadar

Gwadar is a small town almost at the western extreme of Pakistan's coast, close to the Straits of Hormuz and from the sea lanes carrying almost one-third of the global sea-borne oil trade. At one time, it was part of the Sultanate of Oman, which sold it to Pakistan in 1958. Pakistan has been trying to develop Gwadar as a secondary port for decades – most of Pakistan's maritime traffic is handled in Karachi. It also hoped Gwadar would become a regional trans-shipment hub and a gateway to the sea for Afghanistan and Central Asia. Pakistan tried to develop the port on its own, with no success. Later on, it sought China's assistance – in 2001, Pakistan's then dictator Pervez Musharraf raised the matter of Gwadar Port with China's Premier Zhu Rongji during his visit to Beijing.[19] But the project never took off.

In 2007, a consortium led by PSA Singapore was awarded the contract to operate the Gwadar Port for 40 years. Over this period, PSA was to invest $5–8 billion in developing the port, which would, in turn, generate $17–31 billion worth of revenues.[20] This didn't materialise either, and in 2013, the control of the port was handed over to Pakistan's all-weather friend China. China Overseas Port Holding Company, a state-owned enterprise, set up a Pakistani subsidiary that runs the port.

In its latest avatar, the Gwadar Port is a cornerstone project of the $62 billion China–Pakistan Economic Corridor, with investments worth over $1 billion earmarked for the region around the port. Apart from the port, an airport, a highway, a power project and two industrial zones are proposed for the area.[21]

At various points, Pakistan's leaders have cited multiple rationales for Gwadar:

1   As a secondary port for Pakistan, reducing the load on Karachi
2   As a regional trans-shipment hub
3   As an industrial zone, where raw materials are brought in and processed, and finished goods are exported
4   As a way for China to bypass Malacca Straits – for its oil imports and for its exports[22]

Is Gwadar economically viable?

First, the Gwadar region faces severe water shortages, making economic activity difficult. It received just 11.1 mm of total rainfall in 2017[23]: drinking water supplies had to be shipped to Gwadar on a naval tanker on one occasion.[24] Any industrial activity will require significant quantities of fresh water. Desalination is possible, but is energy-intensive and costly – large-scale desalination for industry is possible in energy-rich Persian Gulf, not in Pakistan. Any trans-shipment port in the Arabian Sea will have to compete with Dubai and Colombo and will look at India as a major market. Given Pakistan's state-sponsored terror in India, it is unlikely that India will provide financial support for Gwadar in this way.

Second, Balochistan is Pakistan's largest, poorest and most thinly populated province – it doesn't provide a hinterland which will generate traffic for the port. Any goods coming in will have to be shipped to other parts of Pakistan or further. Most of Pakistan's population lives along the Indus river axis – so any goods coming into Gwadar for Pakistan will have to be put on a truck for shipping to Karachi or Punjab. Gwadar has no rail connectivity to the rest of Pakistan, while the cost of shipping goods via roads for long distances is very high. A long-running insurgency for rights of the Baloch nation, directed against the Pakistani army, makes long distance movement of goods difficult.

Third, Gwadar is not a suitable base for moving oil and other goods to and from China. Pakistan and China are separated by the Karakoram Mountains. The four provinces of China closest to Pakistan – Xinjiang, Tibet, Qinghai and Gansu – together account for about 40% of China's landmass and just 5% of its population. Any oil that is consumed in China will be consumed in more populous provinces such as Sichuan and Yunnan. The cheapest way to move oil on land is via a pipeline. If an oil pipeline is built from Gwadar to interior China, the cost of oil will rise by $8–10 per barrel– perhaps even more if the 14,000 foot elevation at Pakistan–China border is factored in. The cost of shipping oil to Shanghai from Hormuz is $2–3 per barrel at 2019 shipping rates. Moreover, Sichuan and Yunnan are closer to China's own ports such as Shanghai, Shenzhen, Ningbo, Hong Kong, Qingdao and Guangzhou, than they are to China–Pakistan border. From a cost point of view, Gwadar as an oil shipment hub is a non-starter. The same equation will apply, even more so, for shipping cargo from interior China to Pakistan – the cost of putting a container on a train (which isn't there right now) is an order of magnitude higher than putting it on a ship, and a container sent to Pakistan will have to cross a 14,000 mountain range and the entire length of Pakistan as well. Moreover, Pakistan and China don't have year-round connectivity – the Khunjareb pass connecting the two is blocked for 4 months a year.

Figure 3.2 Gwadar Port: Trade Hub or Military Asset
Source: Gateway House

Finally, Gwadar can provide connectivity to Afghanistan – but Afghanistan already has another outlet to the sea –India developed Chabahar Port in Iran, just 172 km to west of Gwadar. Chabahar is a less ambitious project and was handling 8–10 ships every month by 2019 – compared to one ship every month on an average for Gwadar. Afghanistan has a relatively small population of 37 million and is among the lowest income countries in the world – so trade volumes from Afghanistan will not be very large and will be split with Chabahar.

So what is Gwadar good for?

Given that Gwadar doesn't have economic potential, why is China investing heavily in the area?

The answer can be seen in Djibouti in East Africa and Sri Lanka in South Asia. In Sri Lanka, China invested heavily in building infrastructure – funded by high-cost debt. This included almost $1 billion spent on Hambantota in Southern Sri Lanka on a port and an airport. These two have the distinction of being the world's emptiest port and the world's emptiest airport, respectively. The Hambantota

Port, in its initial phase of operations in 2017–2018, was hosting one ship a week on an average – not sufficient to serve the large debt incurred for the port. Eventually, debt became equity and the port had to be handed over to a Chinese company on a 99-year lease – similar to the terms on which Hong Kong was leased to the UK by China over a century ago.

The other example is Djibouti, a small and indebted country – with much of the debt owed to China.[25] Eventually, Djibouti became the host site for China's first overseas military base in 2017.[26] Djibouti again has a sensitive position sitting astride sea lanes connecting the Indian Ocean to the Mediterranean Sea, via the Red Sea and Suez Canal. Djibouti was perhaps the least controversial location for China to host a military base, given that it already has military installations from many other nations. It is also the equivalent of dipping toes into unknown waters – China will follow it up with other military bases – Hambantota and Gwadar could be future military bases for Pakistan.

Gwadar, as mentioned earlier, sits close to the Straits of Hormuz. Over two-thirds of India's oil imports come from the Persian Gulf, and over half of all the oil that India imports is brought in from the Gulf of Kutch. Gwadar is close to these sea lanes (see Figure 3.3). In the future, it could be one way for China to tamper with India's energy flows.

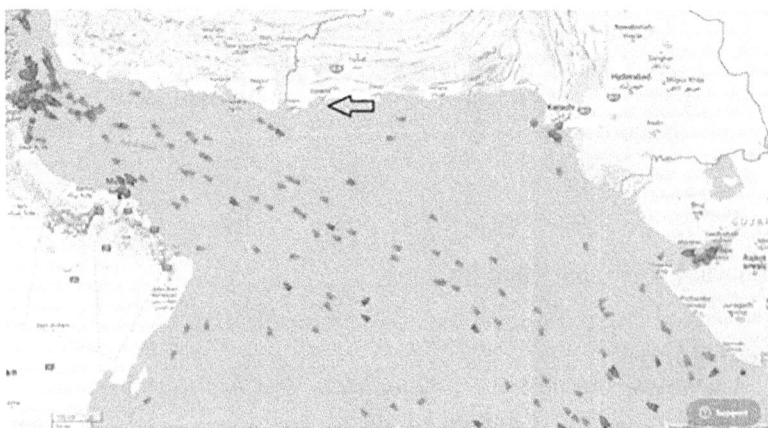

Figure 3.3 Oil Tankers sailing from Persian Gulf to India & the World (www.marinetraffic.com). Note the concentration of ships at the Straits of Hormuz and the Gulf of Kutch.[27]

Gulf of Kutch

If there is one place that can be considered India's energy hub, it is the Gulf of Kutch. It is the closest point in India to West Asia – offering the shortest sailing time. Historically, Kutch has been home to prosperous maritime kingdoms. The Princely State of Kutch, on the northern coast of the Gulf, was one of the longest lasting kingdoms in India, from the early 1500s to 1948. To the south, in the Kathiawar peninsula, was the princely state of Jamnagar – famous for its ruler Jamsahab Ranjit Singh, the cricketer. Another princely state in the Kathiawar peninsula was Porbandar – famous as the birthplace of Mahatma Gandhi, whose family had served the rulers as diwans. While the region is arid and not very suited for agriculture, the coastline and the ports provided the basis for the prosperity of this region. Gujarati merchants were spread along the entire Arabian Sea/Indian Ocean littoral in the British era.

In the present day, apart from the short sailing time to the Persian Gulf, Kutch offers another advantage – it is also the shortest distance an oil pipeline has to travel to reach India's interior – pushing oil through a pipeline is very energy-intensive. As a result, massive investments in oil and gas have come here over the years.

Indian Oil's import terminal, which brings in oil for the Koyali, Mathura and Panipat refineries, is in the Gulf of Kutch. Supertankers are offloaded at a single point mooring; the oil is then pumped into Indian Oil's tank farm, and from there into the Salaya-Mathura pipeline, supplying the other two refineries en route. Together, the three IOC refineries processed 38.7 million tons of petroleum in 2018–2019 – a little under one-fifth of India's total oil consumption.

During the 1990s, Reliance Industries put up its mega refinery in Jamnagar, an old princely state in the Southern part of the Gulf of Kutch. At 27 million tons per annum, this refinery turned India into a net exporter of petroleum products. In the early 2000s, RIL followed this up with a second refinery right next to the existing facility. Close by, in Vadinar, is the third private sector oil refinery – originally built by Essar Oil, now owned by Russia's Rosneft. The two other public sector oil majors – Bharat Petroleum and Hindustan Petroleum, also have oil terminals in Kutch which supply oil to the Bina and Bhatinda refineries of the two companies. In all, close to 150 million tons of crude oil – 3 million barrels/day – two-thirds of India's oil consumption, is imported via the Gulf of Kutch.

Unfortunately, the Gulf of Kutch is right next to Pakistan, posing an immense security risk. Guarding this infrastructure is one of the major objectives for the Indian armed forces.

Malacca dilemma

The Malacca Straits are the shortest route connecting the Indian and the Pacific Oceans. Ships sailing from the Persian Gulf to China, Japan and South Korea must pass through these straits, as must ships sailing from China to West Asia. Malacca Straits are an energy security issue, not for India but for China.

China is now the world's largest oil importer – bringing in almost 10 million barrels/day of oil, almost three-fourth of its total oil consumption. Some of the imports come from Russia and the energy-rich Central Asia, Persian Gulf remains a major contributor. All of this oil has to use the Malacca Straits, and ships can be stopped by accidents, piracy (common in these waters) or hostile action by rival naval powers. China also perceives India as a threat here, with the Andaman and Nicobar islands close to the straits.

China has tried to cut down its vulnerability to the Malacca dilemma in multiple ways. Gwadar Port (see earlier section), has been pitched as one solution to this dilemma but is unworkable. China has also tried other approaches as well.

Strategic petroleum reserves

Like other large economies, China has set up a strategic petroleum reserve. In 2019, together with its SPR, China had about 80 days' worth of oil in storage.[28]Crude oil is typically stored in large circular tanks with floating roofs, big enough to be visible from space (see Figure 3.4). The tanks are of a standard height, and the shadow of the sides of the tank on the roof can be used to gauge how full they are. One of the companies doing just that is Orbital Insight, which provides and analyses geospatial data. In 2016, Orbital Insight used satellite images of China's oil storage farms to estimate that the country had 600 million barrels of oil in storage,[29] more than double the official figure for SPR.

Myanmar oil and gas pipeline

China is the largest investor in Myanmar, as well as the top supplier of weapons to the military regime. Myanmar is rich in oil and gas, but has been avoided by global oil companies because of sanctions – China has been an early investor here. Chinese companies have also invested heavily in Myanmar's hydropower sector – with the dams exporting electricity to China.

Figure 3.4 Oil Storage Tanks at Dalian (Google Earth)[30]

However, Myanmar offers another advantage – the provinces of Yunnan and Sichuan are much closer to the Bay of Bengal than they are to the Pacific Ocean. Better connectivity via Myanmar can help reduce China's dependence on the Malacca Straits. Thus, Myanmar is the focus of much Chinese investment, including the China–Myanmar Economic Corridor, which proposes to build ports, railway lines and oil and gas pipelines connecting China to the Bay of Bengal via Myanmar (see Figure 3.5).

China has already built an oil and gas pipeline connecting the port of Kyaukpyu in Myanmar to Kunming, the capital city of Yunnan province. Oil tankers come in and are offloaded at the Kyaukpyu port, and this oil is pumped a relatively short distance to Kunming. Compared to Gwadar, this pipeline is much shorter – this is less than the distance from Kunming to the Chinese coast. However, this pipeline cuts down only some risks – a more powerful navy that can block access to the Malacca Straits can also cut off access to Kyaukpyu port.

Figure 3.5 Chinese Investments in Myanmar (Gateway House)

Kra canal

Another mega-project, so far mostly in media, is the Kra canal – dug through the Kra Isthmus of Thailand (see Figure 3.6) in the Malay Peninsula, connecting the Andaman Sea with the Gulf of Thailand. Two groups of private investors from China and Thailand signed an MOU in 2015 to build the canal, which would cut transit time for vessels and also bypass the Malacca Straits.[31] The Thai and Chinese governments were quick to deny any official involvement in this project,[32] but it is quite possible that the Chinese government used a private firm as a front to test the waters, and to have plausible deniability. In the case of China, the dividing line between the public and the private sector is often not very clear.

Given the large outlay and the geographic challenge (high elevation of the Kra isthmus) and long time required for execution, Kra is unlikely to be a reality in the foreseeable future (2030). The utility is also limited because access denial to the Malacca Straits will also mean access denial to the Kra canal.

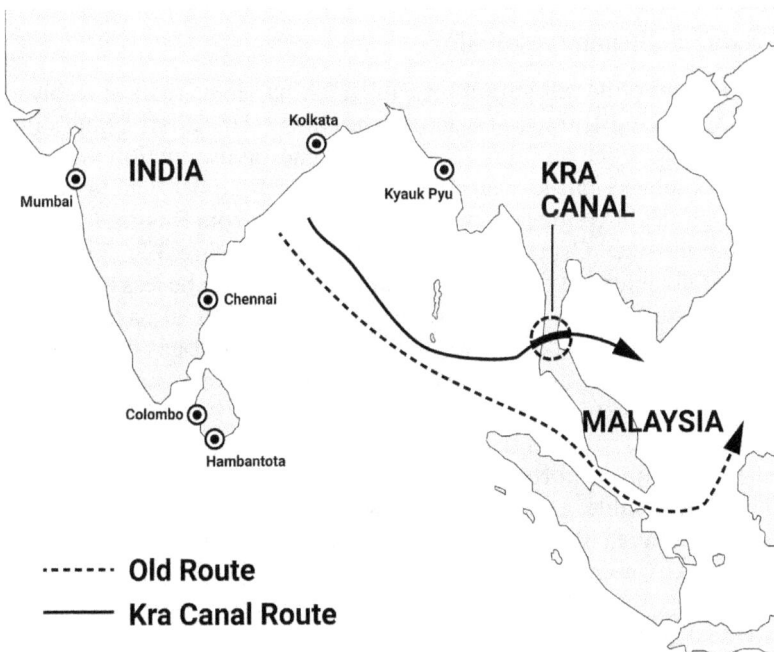

Figure 3.6 Kra Canal[33]

Figure 3.7 Malacca Straits[34]

Malacca dilemma resolved?

As a result of its mitigation measures, China seems to have resolved the Malacca dilemma, at least for the short term. First, China's import dependence on oil is 75% – with domestic production at a very respectable 3.9 million barrels/day. Of the remainder, China is buying significant volumes of oil (and natural gas) from Russia, Kazakhstan and other Central Asian republics (see Figure 3.7). Thus, the actual dependence on West Asia oil for China may be less than 50%. Since China already has oil reserves adding up to 80 days – or 160 days of 50% oil, if oil inflows are reduced to half, it has more than 5 months to adjust to the reduced supply or to find alternatives.

Sailing time from West Asia to Chinese ports is approximately 40 days, 20 days to reach the Malacca Straits, and another 20 days from there to Chinese ports. If, for some reason, the Malacca Straits were no longer usable, at least 20 days' worth of oil imports in tankers in transit between Malacca and China would still reach their destination. This gives China another 3 weeks of buffer. Adding this to the 160 days of buffer (from SPR), China has a good 6 months to find resolutions to the disruption.

Effectively, China has been able to solve the Malacca dilemma. India needs to use a similar approach to reduce risks to its own energy flows.

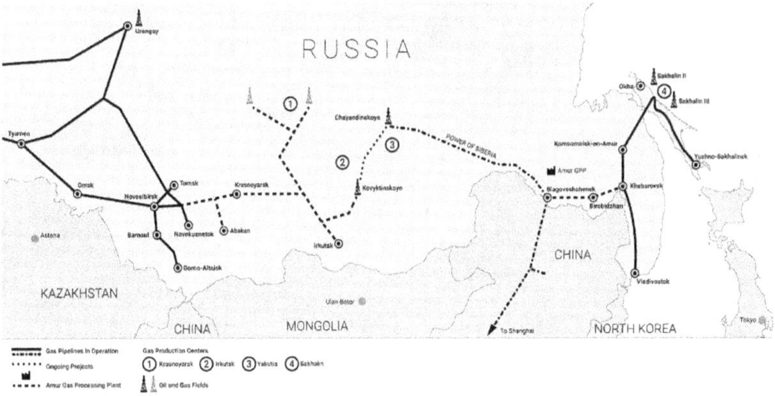

Figure 3.8 Power of Siberia Pipeline (Gazprom)[35]

String of pearls

Gwadar and Kyauk Pyu aren't the only ports being developed by China in the Indian Ocean. A Chinese company is also operating the Hambantota Port – originally built as a part of the One Belt, One Road initiative and had to be subsequently handed over to China for debt repayment. Chinese state-owned companies also own and operate ports in Kenya (Mombasa) and Djibouti – both countries are highly indebted and China is the key creditor. In all, Chinese companies – all government-owned, own and operate at least nine ports in the Indian Ocean region, with more potential investments in Bangladesh, Maldives and Cambodia.

This network of Chinese ports is called 'String of Pearls' in popular media. One of the fears in the Indian strategic community is that some/many of these ports may eventually become military bases, giving China a permanent presence in the Indian Ocean, outside of its home waters, and posing a threat to India's maritime traffic and energy flows. Of key concern to India are the ports of Gwadar (Pakistan), Hambantota (Sri Lanka) and Maldives.

Opinions on string of pearls are mixed. Some military planners scoff at the idea – a maritime base is not just a port where vessels come in for fuel and food. It is also a place where vessels come in for resupply of weapons, and for repairs and maintenance in a place of safety, where they are well defended.

The ports of Hambantota and Gwadar are not connected to China and cannot be defended from there. The home countries – Pakistan

Figure 3.9 Chinese ports in Indian Ocean

and Sri Lanka – cannot defend these ports against Indian air power, which can overwhelm the air forces of these two countries. So it is unlikely that these two ports will become major military bases, though they may host some Chinese military assets, particularly intelligence/listening posts. Also, Gwadar may allow China to maintain its submarines – of which it has over 60 – in the Indian Ocean. A submarine is virtually undetectable in a large expanse of open seas, and having a resupply base in the Indian Ocean increases the potency of China's submarine fleet. While China may not be able to exercise 'control' of the seas, it can still deny free use of the seas to India.

The one port which can host Chinese navy in the conventional sense is Kyauk Pyu in Myanmar, which is geographically close to China's population and industrial centre of Yunnan, and within reach of China's land-based air power.

Notes

1 Timofeev, I. 2018. "The Sanctions against Russia: Escalation Scenarios and Countermeasures." Russia International Affairs Council.
2 Timofeev, I. 2018. "The Sanctions against Russia: Escalation Scenarios and Countermeasures." Russia International Affairs Council.
3 BNP Paribas. 2014. "BNP Paribas announces a comprehensive settlement regarding the review of certain USD transactions by US authorities".https://group.bnpparibas/en/press-release/bnp-paribas-announces-comprehensive-settlement-review-usd-transactions-authorities

4 SocieteGenerale. 2018. "SocieteGenerale Reaches Agreements With U.S. Authorities To Resolve U.S. Economic Sanctions And AML Investigations". https://www.societegenerale.com/en/Newsroom/Societe-Generale-reaches-agreements-with-US-authorities-to-resolve-US-economic-sanctions-and-AML-investigations
5 Department of Justice. 2012. "HSBC Holdings Plc. And HSBC Bank USA N.A. Admit to Anti-Money Laundering and Sanctions Violations, Forfeit $1.256 Billion in Deferred Prosecution Agreement." *Justice.gov*, December 11, 2012. https://www.justice.gov/opa/pr/hsbc-holdings-plc-and-hsbc-bank-usa-na-admit-anti-money-laundering-and-sanctions-violations
6 Arms Control Association. 2019. "The Joint Comprehensive Plan of Action (JCPOA) at a Glance | Arms Control Association." *Armscontrol.org*, 2019. https://www.armscontrol.org/factsheets/JCPOA-at-a-glance
7 Congressional Research Service. 2021. "Venezuela: Overview of U.S. Sanctions." https://fas.org/sgp/crs/row/IF10715.pdf
8 Saudi Press Agency. 2017. "United Arab Emirates Severs Relations with Qatar." https://www.spa.gov.sa/viewstory.php?lang=en&newsid=1637351
9 Saudi Gazette. 2017. "Why 8 Nations Severed Ties with Qatar." *Saudigazette*, June 6, 2017. https://saudigazette.com.sa/article/179949
10 Reuters. 2018. "Saudi Official Hints at Plan to Dig Canal on Qatar Border." *Reuters*, August 31, 2018. https://www.reuters.com/article/us-saudi-qatar-canal/saudi-official-hints-at-plan-to-dig-canal-on-qatar-border-idUSKCN1LG13H
11 Islamic Republic News Agency. 2017. "Iran Exports 180 Tons of Fruits, Vegetables to Qatar." *IRNA English*, June 14, 2017. https://en.irna.ir/news/82565089/Iran-exports-180-tons-of-fruits-vegetables-to-Qatar
12 Islamic Republic News Agency. 2017. "1,100 Tons of Food Products Exported to Qatar Daily from Bushehr." *IRNA English*, June 20, 2017. https://en.irna.ir/news/82571237/1-100-tons-of-food-products-exported-to-Qatar-daily-from-Bushehr
13 Saudi Press Agency. 2019. "Statement by the Ministry of Foreign Affairs." https://www.spa.gov.sa/viewfullstory.php?lang=en&newsid=1969987#1969987
14 Nichols, Michelle. 2020. "Exclusive: U.N. Investigators Find Yemen's Houthis Did Not Carry out Saudi Oil Attack." *Reuters*, January 8, 2020. https://www.reuters.com/article/us-saudi-aramco-attacks-un-exclusive/exclusive-u-n-investigators-find-yemens-houthis-did-not-carry-out-saudi-oil-attack-idUSKBN1Z72VX
15 U.S. Department of Defence. 2020. "Statement by the Department of Defence." https://www.defense.gov/Newsroom/Releases/Release/Article/2049534/statement-by-the-department-of-defense/
16 Central Intelligence Agency. 2007. "Middle East Oil and Gas." Library of Congress. https://www.loc.gov/resource/g7421h.ct002142/
17 Aramco. 2018. "Yanbu South Terminal Export Capacity." https://www.saudiaramco.com/en/news-media/news/2018/yanbu-south-terminal-export-capacity
18 Embassy of the United Arab Emirates. 2012. "Abu Dhabi Crude Oil Pipeline Project". https://www.uae-embassy.org/news-media/abu-dhabi-crude-oil-pipeline-project
19 Dawn. 2008. "Gwadar Port: 'History-Making Milestones.'" *DAWN. COM*, April 14, 2008. https://www.dawn.com/news/297994/gwadar-port-history-making-milestones

20 Aziz, Faisal. 2007. "UPDATE 1-Singapore's PSA Takes over Pakistan's Gwadar Port." *Reuters*, February 6, 2007. https://uk.reuters.com/article/singapore-pakistan/update-1-singapores-psa-takes-over-pakistans-gwadar-port-idUKISL16944320070206

21 Bhandari, Amit, and Chandni Jindal. 2021. "Chinese Investments in Pakistan: Gateway House Map No. 5." Gatewayhouse.in. 2021. https://www.gatewayhouse.in/wp-content/uploads/2018/11/GH_PakistanMap A3-0803-01.png

22 China Overseas Ports Holding Company Pakistan (Pvt.) Ltd. n.d. "COPHC Pakistan." Cophcgwadar.com. http://cophcgwadar.com/about. aspx

23 World Weather Online. n.d. "Gwadar Monthly Climate Averages." WorldWeatherOnline.com. https://www.worldweatheronline.com/gwadar-weather-averages/balochistan/pk.aspx

24 Pakistan Defence. 2017. "Fleet Tanker PNS NASR to Gwadar with 1200 Tons of Fresh/Drinking Water." Pakistan Defence. 2017. https://defence. pk/pdf/threads/fleet-tanker-pns-nasr-to-gwadar-with-1200-tons-of-fresh-drinking-water.497810/

25 International Monetary Fund. Middle East and Central Asia Dept. 2017. "Djibouti : 2016 Article IV Consultation-Press Release; Staff Report; and Statement by the Executive Director for Djibouti." https://www. imf.org/en/Publications/CR/Issues/2017/04/06/Djibouti-2016-Article-IV-Consultation-Press-Release-Staff-Report-and-Statement-by-the-44807

26 Yang, You, and Li Jingyi. 2019. "Djibouti: Chinese Military's First Overseas Support Base." News.cgtn.com. 2019. https://news.cgtn.com/news/3d3d514d7859544d34457a6333566d54/index.html

27 Marine Traffic: Global Ship Tracking Intelligence (n.d.). https://www. marinetraffic.com/en/ais/home/centerx:63.0/centery:23.8/zoom:7

28 Daly, Tom. 2019. "China Has Enough Oil Inventories to Last about 80 Days: NEA." *Reuters*, September 20, 2019. https://www.reuters.com/article/us-china-energy/china-has-enough-oil-inventories-to-last-about-80-days-nea-idUSKBN1W514V

29 Orbital Insight. 2016. "Orbital Insight Measures China Oil Supply With Satellite Imagery Analysis". https://www.globenewswire.com/news-release/2016/09/29/1052941/0/en/Orbital-Insight-Measures-China-Oil-Supply-With-Satellite-Imagery-Analysis.html

30 Google Earth. "Oil Storage Tanks at Dalian." https://earth.google.com/web/@38.97570559,121.88695944,17.82397061a,4783.26279047d,35y,1.88230 332h,0t,0r

31 Liang, Lee Hong. 2015. "Thailand, China Sign Agreement to Construct a New Strategic Kra Canal." *Seatrade Maritime*, May 19, 2015. https://www.seatrade-maritime.com/asia/thailand-china-sign-agreement-construct-new-strategic-kra-canal

32 Hand, Marcus. 2015. "China, Thai Governments Deny Plan to Build Kra Canal." *Seatrade Maritime*, May 20, 2015. https://www.seatrade-maritime.com/asia/china-thai-governments-deny-plan-build-kra-canal

33 Akshay Narang. 2020. "Thailand gives a major shock to China: Scraps Kra Canal plan and drops submarine deals under public pressure". TFI-Post. https://tfipost.com/2020/09/thailand-gives-a-major-shock-to-china-scraps-kra-canal-plans-and-submarine-deals-under-public-pressure/

34 Energy Information Administration. 2017. "World Oil Transport Chokepoints". https://www.eia.gov/international/analysis/special-topics/World_Oil_Transit_Chokepoints
35 Gazprom. 2019. "Developing Gas Resources and Shaping Gas Transmission System in Eastern Russia." www.gazprom.com. https://www.gazprom.com/projects/power-of-siberia/

4 Using market mechanisms for energy security[1]

India's energy security, especially with regard to oil, has largely been government-driven. This runs against the trend of the increasing role of the private sector in the Indian economy post-1992. India's vibrant and well-functioning financial markets are an enormous source of strength – especially compared to the top-down and statist Chinese economy. This strength can be used to increase India's role (and profile) in the global energy trade, in line with India's increasing weight in the physical oil trade. In the longer run, a more central role in the global oil trade will integrate the economies of oil suppliers more closely with India, making India's energy flows more secure and less prone to disruption.

The first part of this book has looked at how the global energy scenario has transformed in the past 20 years – in demand–supply patterns, trade flows and technology. The one constant in this entire period has been the US Dollar, underpinning the global oil trade. Of late, China has started pushing its currency as a challenger to the US Dollar. Can the Indian rupee be the third player in this race?

Dollar domination of the oil trade

Most of the oil trade across the world, physical or paper, is denominated in the US Dollar – a reflection of the greenback's universal acceptability and status as the international currency. The central role of the Dollar dates back to the 1944 Bretton Woods Agreement, which pegged the value of the Dollar to gold and the value of other currencies to the US Dollar. The end of World War II saw a war-weary Great Britain go off the silver standard (use of silver in regular coins) in 1946. The US remained the only major economy that continued to use silver in everyday currency. The US Dollar was a 26.73 g coin, 90% silver (see Figure 4.1) – as were the lower denomination coins of half Dollar, quarter Dollar and dime (ten cents). This made the US Dollar the preferred medium of exchange, including for the oil trade.

DOI: 10.4324/9781003152927-4

Figure 4.1 US Silver Dollar – 26.73 g, 90% Silver

The U.S. currency was first debased in 1965 – when the silver content of American coins was cut to 40% and then in 1969 when the coins went off silver entirely. In 1971, the US government suspended the Dollar-gold conversion, but it continued to remain the default medium of exchange as there were no viable alternatives. The US was the pre-eminent industrial power, the largest economy and trading nation – and the largest consumer and importer of oil. The next largest economies – Japan and Germany – were less than a quarter the size of the US economy. So oil continued to be priced in Dollars, and countries other than the US continued to hold Dollars to pay for their imports. Aiding the Dollar's large role in the oil trade are Saudi Arabia, Kuwait, the UAE and Qatar – all of them are important oil exporters and have for decades pegged their currency to the US Dollar. The currency peg comes on top of large purchases of US military hardware and the American military presence in the Persian Gulf. This is the strongest possible demonstration by oil exporters of their confidence in the US and the Dollar. Investors and speculators across the world also trust the Dollar.

Paper trade – also Dollar-driven

Worldwide, the oil production is almost 100 million barrels/day. The daily financial trade in oil is at least ten times larger, going by the trading volumes on the major commodity exchanges across the world. Besides crude oil, products such as gasoline/petrol, diesel and heating

Table 4.1 Trading Volume of Major Commodity Exchanges (28 February 2019)

	Product	*Volume*
New York	Nymex Crude	1,010
ICE, London	Brent	678
INE (Shanghai)	Shanghai Crude	256.6
MCX (Mumbai)	Nymex Crude	12.2
Trade volume for Crude oil in million barrels/day.		

oil – which are derived from petroleum – are also traded. Companies and consumers use financial instruments to protect themselves against fluctuations in energy prices. Oil-producing companies, thousands of them in the US, commonly use financial instruments to secure guaranteed prices for future oil production. This ensures that even if oil prices collapse, as they did in early 2016 and then in early 2020, companies will be able to meet costs such as interest payments. The airline industry, for example, commonly uses financial instruments as hedges against price fluctuations, since fuel is a major operating cost. As of now, the three top exchanges for oil trading are New York, London and Shanghai. New York and London have run for decades, while the Shanghai exchange began operations in 2018. Oil is also traded on the Mumbai exchange, though its volume is far lower than on the other three exchanges.

At first glance, the volume of trading on the INE Shanghai seems to be in the same range as the London and New York commodity exchanges. However, the numbers mislead. The Shanghai exchange is much more limited. It is so far limited to crude oil and has recently introduced a second energy product – low sulphur fuel oil. Crude oil is just one of the dozens of energy products traded on the New York and London exchanges. Fuels such as natural gas, fuel oil and other petroleum products such as gasoline (petrol) and diesel are also traded on the Western exchanges. These commodities are how oil gets used by end user and are important for any producer/consumer trying to hedge against price fluctuations. Unlike the Western exchanges, the INE doesn't have put/call options at this point – also required for hedging.

Forex reserves: Dollar heavy

As the Dollar is the basis for international trade, including the oil trade, governments and central banks keep the bulk of their foreign exchange reserves in the US Dollar. Countries across the world had

Table 4.2 Trend in Global Foreign Exchange Reserves

	1999	2009	2019
US Dollar	979.8	2,848.3	6,745.6
Euro	247.0	1,269.6	2,275.9
Yuan	0.0	0.0	217.7
British Pound	87.9	133.0	631.4
Yen	39.8	194.9	511.8
Others	25.2	137.5	695.9
Total	1,379.7	4,583.3	11,078.4

Source: IMF. Figures in $ billion.

over $11 trillion in their forex reserves by the end of 2019, of which 61% or $6.7 trillion was in US Dollars. There have been sharp increases in forex reserves held around the world in the past 20 years – after-effects of the East Asian crisis of 1997 and the Western financial crisis of 2008. Most of this increase has been in the US Dollar holdings.

How America gains from the Dollar

The use of the Dollar as the international medium of exchange and reserve currency gives the US several advantages. Since other countries want to hold US securities, the cost of borrowing for the US government and consumers is less than what it would otherwise be. This is a major benefit for the debt-fuelled consumption that drives the American economy. By holding large volumes of US currency and securities as foreign exchange reserves, other countries subsidise the US government and consumers. The benefits of owning the global reserve currency go beyond cheaper borrowing costs, however.

Geopolitical use of reserve currency

Financial dominance also benefits the US geopolitically. Since most international trade is denominated in Dollars, almost all international transactions pass through the US banking system at some point. The US can withdraw this access from a country by imposing sanctions, hitting the economy of any target country. The US has imposed unilateral sanctions in the recent past on Russia, Venezuela and Iran. In all three cases, sanctions resulted in major economic disruptions for the target economies, including currency devaluation, loss of export markets and economic slowdowns. While the US reaps the geopolitical benefits from the Dollar's dominance, countries such as India are often left bearing the costs. Russia, Iran and Venezuela are all oil-rich countries and are important oil exporters, including India. India has large investments in the Russian oil industry. Sanctions on these countries force countries like India to make the unpalatable choice between losing major suppliers and being denied access to the US banking system. Sanctions also reduce the amount of oil available in the world market, pushing up prices. The price of crude oil rose from under $40/barrel in 2016 to almost $70/barrel in 2019 – sanctions on major oil producers/exporters were one reason for the spike. In the case of Russia, US sanctions also reduced India's ability to import critical defence hardware. The three branches of India's armed forces rely on Russian-origin military equipment. Virtually all of Russia's major defence manufacturers are currently under US sanctions – potentially cutting India off from new hardware as well as spares and supplies for existing equipment.

Regulation as a tool for geopolitical leverage

Since the 2008 financial crisis, US regulators have found a number of corporations guilty of violating American law, forcing them to pay fines running into billions of Dollars. In some cases, the targeted companies were American and the action was justified as needing to protect the global financial system – for instance, fines imposed for misselling mortgage-backed securities (Bank of America, JP Morgan, Citigroup and Goldman Sachs). In other cases, the US action targeted foreign companies for causing environmental damage within the US–BP for the Gulf of Mexico oil spill[2] and Volkswagen for falsifying emission data.[3]

The third group of companies was punished for violating geopolitically motivated US sanctions in what might be considered a form of regulatory extortion (BNP Paribas, HSBC). In many cases, companies agreed to pay the penalties to buy peace rather than get into potentially ruinous litigation with the US government; one example is BNP Paribas,[4] which agreed to pay $8.9 billion to the US.

In some of these cases, especially those linked to sanctions, the companies had not broken any law in their home countries. However, the threat of losing access to the US banking system would have finished them as viable commercial entities, so they were willing to pay large fines. For some departments of the US government, these fines have become a source of revenue.

Virtually all of these mega fines have been levied since 2010. With several of India's oil suppliers under sanctions, there is an increasing risk that an Indian oil company may get caught violating American law – and end up paying heavy fines.

Is the status quo changing?

The dominance of the Dollar in international transactions results from the dominance of the US economy. But the rise of Asia – in particular, China and India – represents a challenge to the Dollar's supremacy. China is now the second largest economy in the world, having grown from the equivalent of 6% of the US economy in 1990 to 66% in 2018.[5] Over the same period, India has grown from the equivalent of 5% of the American economy to 13%. China, and eventually India, are each projected to overtake the US economy in sheer size.[6]

While the US is now less enthusiastic about globalisation than in the past, China is pushing ahead with it, advocating its own version of free trade and promoting institutions such as the Asian Infrastructure Investment Bank (AIIB) and the New Development Bank (NDB) as alternatives to the IMF and World Bank. These are filling gaps created by the 2008 financial crisis, which raised questions about the sustainability of the Western-centred global financial system.

The oil market has seen a shift too. While the US remains the world's top consumer of oil, it is no longer the largest importer, having dropped behind China because of its substantial shale oil production. Japan and the major European economies consume less oil today than they did in 1990, even though global consumption has risen. China is now the world's second largest oil consumer, followed by India.

These two are now the largest and third largest importers of oil worldwide.

The changing structure of the world economy makes alternatives to the Dollar and the US-dominated financial system possible.

Alternatives to the Dollar: early challengers

The first global challenge to the Dollar's dominance came from the Euro, which was created in 1999. The Eurozone is the world's second largest economic bloc after the US, and includes economic heavyweights such as Germany, France and Italy. Like the US, the Eurozone is a democratic area governed by rule of law and transparent regulation – key requirements for foreigners to trust a currency. Since its inception, the Euro has gained market share and now accounts for 20% of global foreign exchange reserve holdings. But it still lags the Dollar by a wide margin (refer Table 2).

The Euro is unlikely to progress much further as an alternative because of multiple factors.

1   **Economic Problems with key members:** Some European economies are struggling under heavy public debt. Greece, Portugal and Italy have debt-to-GDP ratios exceeding 100%. In the case of Italy, Spain, Portugal and Greece, the current GDP (2018) is lower than the 2008 figures.

2   **Brexit:** Britain, which was a part of the European Union but not the Eurozone, has voted to withdraw from the union. The confusion surrounding Brexit is unlikely to increase public confidence in the Euro.

Over the last 20 years, governments hostile to the US and facing American sanctions also attempted to break away from the Petro-Dollar dominance. Specifically:

1   In the early 2000s, Iraq decided to price its crude oil exports in Euros instead of Dollars.[7]

2   China and Russia have moved part of their oil trade from the Dollar to their respective currencies. The large volume of Chinese exports to Russia makes this possible. Wide-ranging US sanctions on Russia have catalysed this trade.

3   During the earlier US sanctions on Iran, India paid for Iranian crude in rupees via Turkish and European banks without exposure to the US financial system. Because of the imbalance in trade between the two countries, Iran was left with a large amount in Indian rupees – which could only be used to buy Indian goods, demonstrating that the practice was only viable as a short-term stopgap.

4   Venezuela tried to sidestep US sanctions on its oil industry by introducing the 'Petro', a cryptocurrency. This is considered a failure.

Oil exporters sanctioned by the US have tried to find alternative markets, rather than seeking an alternative financial architecture. These don't represent a challenge to the Dollar's status as a basis for the world oil trade, but such activity shows that if there were an alternative to the US Dollar for trading oil, there would be a ready base of customers.

   The challenge from China is of a different nature, and far more credible than any of the scattershot measures tried in the past. China is now the world's second largest economy, and has started projecting itself as a rival to the US on numerous fronts, including by trying to encourage the use of the Yuan as an international medium of exchange, in oil trade as well.

The petro-yuan challenge

China's challenge to the US is probably the most significant one the US has faced since 1945, is occurring at the economic, military, technological and financial levels. China's economy is expected to overtake the US economy in size by 2030, and institutions it launched, such as the AIIB and the NDB, are meant to rival the US-dominated IMF and World Bank. China is mounting a military challenge to the US through its naval building, creation and weaponisation of artificial islands and assertion of expansive territorial claims over its neighbours – many of whom are America's allies. It has unveiled 'China 2030', by which it seeks to become the world leader in emerging technologies such as artificial intelligence, robotics, aviation and space.[8]

China's financial challenge to the US rests on three strategies:

1   Influencing global financial architecture by acquiring stakes in systemically important companies and institutions. Examples of this include acquisitions of stakes in the Karachi and Dhaka stock exchanges and the acquisition of the Standard Bank in South Africa.
2   Exporting Chinese standards and influence via the Belt and Road Initiative (BRI) and AIIB and NDB
3   Supplanting the US Dollar in the world oil trade by using China's recent status as the world's largest oil importer

The focus of this chapter is only on the third Chinese objective listed here – to replace the US Dollar with the Chinese Yuan for the global oil trade.

Is the petro-yuan real or speculative?

In March 2018, China launched oil futures on the Shanghai-based International Energy Exchange (INE) – a possible first step towards shifting the global oil trade to the Yuan from the US Dollar. By the end of 2018, this exchange reached a daily traded volume of over 500 million barrels[9] – less than half the volume of Brent[10] or WTI,[11] but far ahead of all other global exchanges. On this metric – trading volume – petro-yuan became very successful in a very short span of time. But a deeper dive into these numbers shows that this trade is quite shallow.

On January 18, 2019, a typical day, a total of 523,136 contracts for 1,000 barrels were traded on the INE. Of this, more than 98% – 516,038 contracts – were for a single contract (March 2019). This indicates that the trading in Shanghai initially was almost entirely speculative. If an oil-producing company wants to hedge its future revenues, it will do so in line with future production – so it will go for a mix of futures contracts expiring over several months. Similarly, if a large consumer of oil, such as an airline, wants to hedge future fuel expenses, it will again use a mix of futures contracts of varying maturities, to match actual consumption. If almost all the trading on an exchange arises from a single contract, that means actual producers and consumers are playing a minimal role and the trading volume is being driven by speculators. If oil producers/consumers are absent, the exchange serves no higher purpose – it is just a platform for speculation.

This trading pattern may be shifting. On June 18, 2020, the total traded volume in the Shanghai crude contract was 198,352 – or 198 million barrels. Of this total, 74.3% of the volume was for the July contract while 19.7% was for the August contract – meaning 95% of the total trade. However, 5% of the trade was for other contracts, meaning the trading pattern may be spreading. However, it is still too early to judge clearly.

A second metric to judge an exchange is the delivery volume or the number of physical barrels actually delivered at the expiry of the contract. For the first INE contract, the delivery volume was 601,000 barrels of oil – less than one-third the volume of oil carried by a supertanker and less than one-tenth of China's daily oil imports. In one of the subsequent months after launch, settlement volume fell to just 8,000 barrels. Settlement volumes have subsequently risen, but sharp fluctuations from one month to the next make it difficult to spot a clear trend.

Average holding time is a third metric. Data compiled by a wire agency in mid-2018 showed that the average holding time for a contract in Shanghai was 2 hours, compared to 65 hours for a Brent contract.[12]

The low delivery volume, the disproportionate role of a single contract and lower holding time all indicate that the exchange in Shanghai is being used mostly for speculation. The investors could be China's retail investors, who were heavily burned as the stock market by 2018 had fallen nearly 50% from its 2015 level (30% during 2018 alone). Some of the speculation taking place on the stock exchange may have migrated to the commodity exchange.

Another factor impeding the petro-yuan's rise and the INE becoming a global trading hub is that foreign traders, users and consumers are likely to stay away from the Chinese exchange. They were chastened by the Chinese government's heavy-handed intervention after the 2015 stock market meltdown when it used threats to force investors and short-sellers to buy and hold even though they wanted to sell.[13] Foreign traders and companies who are already trading on other global markets are unlikely to patronise an exchange on which they cannot trade freely or withdraw funds at will. There is the additional issue of transparency and reliability of data coming out of China – can a critical price benchmark for the world economy come from an unreliable source? This unwillingness to take large bets on a Chinese exchange will increase after COVID-19 pandemic – which has shown an aggressive China that has tried to cover up serious problems with global repercussions.

Petro-yuan: issues for India

China's increasingly aggressive behaviour, more so after the outbreak of the COVID-19 pandemic, is a growing concern for India. In June 2020, a confrontation between Indian and Chinese armies at the Ladakh border resulted in the death of 20 Indian soldiers – the Chinese side suffered casualties but didn't release any figures. This confrontation could have been an attempt by China to change facts on the ground while India was preoccupied with the pandemic. China is putting pressure on India on other fronts as well:

1   **BRI:** China has pushed many of India's neighbours into a debt trap, making them economically and politically dependent on Beijing. Also, the China Pakistan Economic Corridor (CPEC), a part of the BRI, passes through the Indian Territory under illegal Pakistani occupation. China may use assets created under the BRI to create a military presence in Pakistan.
2   **Political and Economic Support for Pakistan:** China provides political and economic support to Pakistan, enabling that country to pursue state-backed terrorism against India. China's repeated blocking of the UN resolution on Pakistan-based terrorist Masood Azhar fits into this pattern.
3   **Military presence in the Indian Ocean:** Chinese navy ships and submarines are increasingly patrolling the Indian Ocean – and have often made port calls in regional ports. China started its first overseas military base in Djibouti in 2017.

Given China's hostility towards its eastern neighbours (Japan, Philippines, Taiwan and Vietnam) and India, apprehension about a more powerful China with influence over the global oil markets is justified. It will not be in India's interest if the economies of its top oil suppliers, such as the UAE and Saudi Arabia, become more closely integrated with China.

A larger role for the Yuan internationally will first make China immune to sanctions, and may then place it in a position to impose sanctions of its own. The replacement of the US Dollar by the Yuan is not an issue for the US alone; it will also pose a problem for India.

Petro-rupee: the opportunity for India

The shifting global energy balance and the US–China confrontation can create an opportunity for India to advance its role in global finance and give non-Western countries an alternative to the Petro-Dollar. India can make itself the hub of a vibrant new international oil market where oil is traded in rupees. Besides enhancing India's global standing, such a transformation can promote India's national interests by addressing its long-standing vulnerability to energy price fluctuations and building up an SPR at no cost to the taxpayer.

The idea of the Indian rupee as an international currency is not very far-fetched. During the British era, the Indian economy was the largest in the Indian Ocean rim and the British Indian silver rupee was either the currency or formed the basis for the currency of several other countries. As early as the 1850s, Burma used a silver Kyat coin identical to the British Indian silver rupee in weight and purity. The colonial empires of Italy (Somaliland) and Germany (German East Africa) and Portugal (Goa) used coins that were patterned on the Indian rupee. The new Saudi Riyal, introduced in 1935, was also based on the INR. Even after India stopped using silver in coinage (1945), the Reserve Bank of India printed a special 'Gulf Rupee' – for use in the United Arab Emirates, Oman, Kuwait and Bahrain – none of which had a currency of their own at the time. In line with India's relative economic decline and inward looking economic policies after 1947, the international profile of the Indian rupee also fell. Because of repeated devaluations of the Indian rupee, the smaller Gulf states eventually introduced their own currencies in 1969.

This section presents a detailed strategy for achieving these goals. Since the strategy hinges on reshaping energy markets, it is necessary to briefly review India's struggle to address its energy challenges.

Challenge: India's dependence on imported energy

India is now the world's second largest importer of all energy, and the third largest importer of crude oil. Imports account for more than 80% of its oil consumption and are likely to satisfy all of the growth in India's oil demand in the foreseeable future. From 4 million barrels a day

Figure 4.2 Silver Rupee Coins of British India, Portuguese Goa, German East Africa and Burma – Identical in Weight (11.66 g) and Purity (91.7% Silver)

currently, India's oil imports are expected to reach 10 million barrels a day by 2040.[14]

India has long struggled to ensure its access to sufficient supplies of energy at a fair price to feed its growing economy. Today, with annual imports of 1.58 billion barrels and growing, the problem persists. India also struggles with a related issue – having sufficient petroleum reserves to tide itself over short-term disruptions caused by conflicts or other events – such as the attack on Saudi Aramco in September 2019.

The problem is no longer a long-term shortage of oil, as seen in earlier chapters. The problem today is price – and its tendency to fluctuate sharply. India's problems in 1973–1974, 1979–1980 and 1991–1992 had to do with the price of oil, not its availability. The record high oil prices of 2006–2007 did not cause an economic crisis like the past as India had the ability to pay. More recently, the fall in oil price from over $100 per barrel in 2014 to less than $50 per barrel in 2016 was a big relief, enhancing the country's ability to spend on much-needed domestic development. A price spike in September–October 2018 to $85 per barrel again caused concern that the government may roll back deregulation of oil prices and bring back administered prices again – bringing back price distortions that have plagued the Indian economy. India is a consumption driven economy, and a $50 per barrel fall in oil price, multiplied by 1.5 billion barrels, effectively puts $75 billion in the hands of consumers, companies and the government – a massive stimulus to the economy. Conversely, a higher price represents a drain of money, from consumers, companies and also the government.

India can adopt two strategies to protect itself from high and fluctuating energy prices: It can acquire oil fields overseas or use financial markets to hedge against high prices.

It has been acting on the first approach for nearly two decades now. India has made more than 50 investments in oil and gas fields across the world, covered in detail in Chapter 2. But even after 20 years, these investments still account for less than 10% of India's total imports, while requiring large amounts of capital.

The low level of such investments reflects the limitations of this approach. Oil-rich countries such as Saudi Arabia and Kuwait don't permit foreign ownership of oil fields, while some other oil-rich nations – Venezuela and Sudan, for instance – are not good investment prospects because of internal political issues, as Indian companies have discovered to their cost. Iran, though rich in oil and gas, is under severe US sanctions and out of bounds for oil companies, as discussed in Chapter 3. All of this puts a large share of global oil reserves out of reach for Indian investors.

Since India can't meet its entire energy-import needs for the foreseeable future, or even a large part of them, by acquiring overseas reserves alone, it must consider using financial markets to cover the risk of rising energy prices. It is a proven strategy. Companies across the world use energy futures and options to cover the risk of high prices (or low price in the case of oil producers), as do some governments, including Mexico,[15,16] Uruguay[17] and Jamaica.[18]

Energy trade on global commodity exchanges (London and New York) is large and liquid enough to permit India to use them to cover its risk. But using these exchanges poses two problems:

1   The benchmarks for oil traded on these exchanges – Brent and WTI – don't correspond to India's import mix. The need for a more representative indicator has been flagged in the past. There have been accusations in the past that these benchmarks have been manipulated. While the accusations have not been proven or refuted conclusively, they do raise concerns. The negative price for WTI in April 2020 also shows the need for a more representative benchmark.

2   Taking a large position in a foreign financial market can prove politically difficult for the Indian government (or a government-controlled entity). Even if designed to promote energy security, such

an investment can easily be seen as 'speculative' or as a scam in India's charged political environment.

An alternative

An alternative is at hand that can avoid these problems and enable India to weather sharp fluctuations in oil prices and enhance its status in the global economic order. India must shift part of the global oil trade to the rupee and base it on an Indian exchange. This trade will have spin-off benefits for India's government, corporate and financial sectors, and most importantly, its public. In 2013, Gateway House advocated developing new, Asia-centric benchmarks for oil and using financial markets to hedge India's oil imports. While those suggestions targeted specific segments of the energy-finance chain, current conditions call for a more ambitious effort to shifting a part of the whole energy value chain to India.

The building blocks required for this new initiative are already in place: India has three commodity exchanges where futures and options are actively traded. It now has to make these instruments long-term and advance them from being just paper trades to contracts backed by buyers and sellers of physical products.

Shifting a portion of the global oil trade to an Indian energy exchange governed by Indian laws and regulations, where trading would occur in rupees, can bring a number of benefits to India:

1   The Indian government and companies can hedge their exposure to price hikes and other energy price fluctuations.
2   A new oil benchmark can be created that more accurately represents changing consumption patterns and India's own energy requirements.
3   Large-scale energy trade in India can create tens of thousands of high-paying finance and ancillary jobs – as the two stock exchanges have done in Mumbai.
4   The physical delivery of oil and gas traded on the exchange will necessitate the creation of large-scale storage facilities, which can serve as a de facto strategic petroleum reserve to use in an emergency. If the government sets up such a reserve with its own (public) money, it will tie up billions of Dollars of public funds.

What follows is an assessment of the opportunities and risks, and the way to create such an exchange.

Enabling factors

Structural: Economic heft and oil consumption are both shifting towards Asia, with India playing an important role. India is expected to be a major source of growth in global oil demand over the next two decades. Its clout is increased further because the current abundance of hydrocarbons gives buyers more leverage over sellers than in the past. India sits close to West Asia, which has the world's top oil exporters and straddles the sea routes carrying oil to three other top importers – China, Japan and South Korea. India is also an important exporter of refined petroleum products – from two large refineries in Gujarat (Jamnagar and Vadinar in the Gulf of Kutch). This can be the location for an international physical trading hub.

A factor that increases the possibility of this is that India's ties with West Asian oil exporters are changing as India has started investing in oil fields (Oman and the UAE) and some of these countries (Saudi Arabia and the UAE) are investing in India's downstream energy infrastructure. India has invested in other oil-exporting nations, including in Russia, Mozambique and Colombia, although this portfolio is much smaller than China's overseas energy investments.

Legal and Regulatory: India has well-functioning and well-regulated financial markets, unlike China, where the government interfered heavy-handedly to stem a fall in the stock market. Also, unlike China, India does not restrain its private sector, which now dominates several sectors of the economy. The rule of law is applied evenly in India – again, a contrast to China, which in 2019 arrested three Canadian citizens on political grounds (and who remain imprisoned as of 30th June 2020). India also has functioning commodity exchanges, and the markets regulator, the Securities and Exchange Board of India (SEBI), has removed restrictions on commodity options. Commodity futures are now actively traded on the Multi Commodity Exchange (MCX), National Commodity and Derivatives Exchange Limited (NCDEX) and the National Stock Exchange (NSE). MCX and NCDEX also enable trade in commodity options. Crude oil futures and options are both available on the MCX for trading – albeit only very short-term (one or two months) – as opposed to the longer-term contracts (6, 12 and 24 months) that physical hedgers seek. However, current trading volume indicates that there is significant interest in the product from the financial community.

Hurdles

The enabling factors are necessary, but not sufficient to create a vibrant energy trade. Several gaps need to be filled:

1   As an oil importer, India has mostly oil buyers and very few sellers (ONGC, Oil India and Vedanta). For an energy trading platform/ market to be successful, more sellers are needed. As India imports nearly 85% of its crude oil requirement, participation of foreign oil producers in this exchange is a must. This is also true for natural gas.

2   Government interference in financial markets or with regulatory structure – such as the retrospective tax cases filed against Vodafone and Cairn India – can keep away traders and investors. Market participants require certainty and predictability of regulation, which is not always assured in India.

3   Through its various arms – ONGC, Gail India, the Indian Oil Corporation (IOC), Bharat Petroleum Corporation (BPCL) and Hindustan Petroleum Corporation (HPCL) – the Indian government controls most of the country's oil and gas sector: 71% of oil production,[19] 65% of petroleum refining capacity[20] and more than 90% of the retail network. Government owned oil marketing companies (IOC, BPCL and HPCL) have no incentive to use financial markets as they are naturally hedged: they buy crude oil and sell petroleum products, so the cost of oil for them is only a pass through. These firms are also reluctant to engage in an activity that can be seen as speculative. Privately-owned firms are more willing to use financial market mechanisms to cover their risks. The limited role of private companies in the energy sector hinders the creation of a market for energy. Moreover, just three firms – Reliance, Nayara Energy (formerly Essar) and Vedanta (formerly Cairn) – account for more than 95% of private sector participation in the oil sector. The US market, by contrast, has no government oil companies and thousands of micro- to mega-sized private sector firms.

4   Natural gas produced in India is allocated to priority sectors – fertiliser and city gas distribution, and the price is set by the government, not by local demand and supply.[21] A market cannot function without free pricing; India's newly opened Indian Gas Exchange may face this issue.

5   The Indian rupee is not fully convertible. This poses an issue for foreign participants on an Indian exchange because it complicates the remittance of any profits.
6   While crude oil and natural gas are traded on MCX, the trade currently is entirely speculative, as it is in China. Over 90% of the trading volume in a single day's trade is typically for the contract closest to expiry, while there is often zero trade in the contract for 3 months ahead. Oil producers and end users need to be brought into the market.

The road ahead

Creating confidence among foreign investors through assurances that the government will not interfere is not an active measure. It can only be done passively – by not interfering. Among the public sector oil majors, only one – BPCL, is a potential candidate for privatisation. However, the timing will depend on multiple factors – how quickly the world economy recovers from COVID, state of global oil market and India's domestic political dynamics.

Here is how the transition could happen:

Step 1: Invite private participation in India's SPRs through the introduction of crude oil Exchange Traded funds
Step 2: Introduce long-duration futures/options
Step 3: Introduce new products
Step 4: Invite greater foreign participation in India's energy market
Step 5: Government Hedging

Step 1: Crude oil ETF and the SPR

Indians have invested in gold for thousands of years, but recently, they also have the option of buying 'paper gold' – shares in an Exchange Traded Fund that buys and stores gold in a repository on behalf of retail investors. Small investors can buy and sell this gold freely on the stock market, improving their liquidity. While selling physical gold has always involved transaction costs for small investors – including a discount to its true value, which depends on the buyer's discretion, there are no such costs to buying and selling paper gold.

Similar benefits could be created through mutual funds for crude oil ETFs. The actual oil could be held in the SPR (or elsewhere), with ownership resting with the ETF. Investors holding units of the ETF would have ownership of that oil. They could then write long-duration call options in return for a fee, and also sell this oil in the futures market, if they so desire. For instance, an investor with a title to 1,000 barrels of crude oil could sell a future (or a call option) for 6 to 12 months down the line in return for a premium (fee). If oil prices fall sharply (as they did in early 2020), investors will start buying and the volume of oil in storage will increase, which should help stabilise the market. This oil in storage can be used during an emergency – and will serve the same purpose as SPR.

India's SPR, currently at 38 million barrels and due to be expanded by an additional 47 million barrels to cover 21 days of oil imports – represents a good opportunity for such investment. After the planned expansion, the reserves will total 85 million barrels and will cover over $3 billion at current prices.[22] Some of this SPR was filled up when oil price was over $80 per barrel – with oil prices down to $40 per barrel in mid-2020, this also represents a notional loss to the exchequer. The volume of oil required in storage will go up in line with India's energy demand as the SPR tries to increase the number of days covered (90 days is the norm for the International Energy Agency member states). Having part of the SPR owned by investors will save the government money and can also help create a vibrant commodity market in India.

This step will not be politically difficult, and it will create an immediate benefit by freeing up government funds that otherwise will be needed to create the SPR.

Step 2: Long-term futures/options

Once the crude ETF has a large enough pool of subscribers, long-dated options and futures can be introduced on the exchange. These contracts should be designed to allow physical delivery at certain designated oil storage sites (such as the SPR where the oil is held and major oil landing terminals). Since ETF owners will form one part of the trade on the exchange, this will not be speculative, unlike the current trading in financial instruments related to oil. Moreover, the owners of oil ETF shares can make some returns from their assets by selling call options on them; this will allow them to get returns without selling their entire holding. This can be a useful way to reward investors who are holding the SPR at their cost, instead of the government.

Step 3: Introduce new products

While crude oil trade captures most attention, it is unusable by itself. Before it can be used as a fuel, it must be processed into products such as diesel, petrol and aviation fuel. The 4 million-plus barrels that India imports every day are processed into these and other useful products at almost 20 public and private sector oil refineries in India. Unless the consumers of these products also hedge themselves, crude oil futures/ options will have limited utility.

Thus, the next step, after crude oil futures are introduced, should be to launch futures and options for products that are consumed by large-scale oil users like airlines and big road transport companies. Fuel cost is the major operating expense for such businesses, and sudden spikes can hurt profitability. Airlines in the US and Europe routinely hedge their fuel costs.[23] There is no reason why Indian airlines will not do the same, given the opportunity. Oil refineries can sell part of their output to such customers in the futures market and buy a corresponding volume of crude oil (also in the futures market), thus locking in profits today. This will help deepen and broaden the financial market.

Step 4: Foreign/private participation

In the longer run, India needs to bring in foreign oil producers (and traders) to participate in this market. Rosneft is already invested in India, via the Essar Refinery. Saudi Aramco and Abu Dhabi National Oil Company (ADNOC) both have a stake in the proposed 60 million tonne oil refinery at Ratnagiri, Maharashtra. Clearly, oil sellers are interested in demand security, just as India has tried to seek supply security in the past. These companies plan to sell oil to their India-based refining ventures. Part of this trade can be shifted to the energy exchange to provide price visibility and transparency.

Government-owned oil producer ONGC and refiners IOC/BPCL could also be persuaded to sell/purchase a small part of their future production/requirement (3, 6 and 12 months from now) on the exchange to facilitate price discovery and improve the liquidity of the market. For instance, as long as ONGC is selling its oil output within India, the company should not be concerned about whether the oil is headed into storage or into a refinery. Similarly, if IOC is buying oil, it doesn't matter whether the oil is coming from a storage depot or directly from the oil field.

Judging from their long-standing aversion to financial markets, public sector companies are unlikely to participate in this market beyond their clearly defined mandate from the government. So the best option is to reduce the role of the public sector. The proposed refinery at Ratnagiri should be set up as a joint venture company (like Petronet LNG), where the public sector stake is capped at 50%, so that it doesn't operate like a government firm. Such a firm will find it easier to use financial instruments to hedge its exposure to high oil prices, and thus provide much-needed volume/liquidity needed to establish a credible Indian energy benchmark.

Step 5: Government hedging

This is potentially the most complex part of the whole process. The Indian government continues to subsidise the uses of liquefied petroleum gas (LPG) and kerosene. When oil prices were over $100 per barrel, the government also subsidised diesel and petrol users. If oil prices move up sharply, the Indian government will intervene to insulate consumers from the spike; when oil prices crossed $80 per barrel in late 2018, for instance, the government was prepared to step in to keep retail prices stable. The government can hedge this risk on the exchange. Mexico already does this. An oil exporter, it needs a certain price to balance its budget. Therefore, the Mexican government hedges[24] the price at which it sells oil to protect itself against any downturns below that level. The Indian government needs to do the same to protect itself as a buyer from price spikes.

The price at which the Indian government will intervene needs to be set – and the government needs to buy call options at that strike price. This will require expertise the government may not have at the moment – including a good understanding of the energy industry, market movements and how to trade on them. The finance units of the public sector oil companies are the most conversant with these issues, so they should be brought in for their expertise. Ideally, this activity should be carried out by a purpose built entity with a clear goal – to protect the Indian economy from the ill effects of having to pay $100 per barrel for oil. The money spent on hedging should be seen as an insurance premium – a small down payment to protect against a major potential disaster, rather than as an investment.

Conclusion

The first three strategic recommendations proposed in this chapter – inviting private participation in creating an SPR, using this to create a vibrant market in oil futures/options and introducing new products – are very achievable, even considering India's political constraints. The success of subsequent recommendations – bringing in foreign players, reducing the role of government in the oil sector and hedging the government's risk from oil prices, will depend on successful execution and implementation of the first three, together with the political will to act. These are long-term steps that don't need to be acted upon immediately.

The reasons to act are compelling. High oil prices have always hurt India's growth. There is now a chance to guard against that risk using Indian financial markets. With its economic dynamism, strong growth prospects, political stability and well-regulated financial markets, Indian can regain its historical position as the economic nerve centre of the entire region.

Financial markets with credible benchmarks and standards represent one area where India can successfully compete against China. It can't outbid China on infrastructure and it can't outspend China on aid. But India's open markets and rule of law are strong competitive assets that should be fully utilised. If it doesn't act now, it risks ceding this field, where it has an advantage, to China as well. If it does act, the petro-rupee could become a reality and India will take its rightful place as a leading player in global financial markets, alongside the Petro-Dollar.

Notes

1 This chapter is a modified version of Amit Bhandari's "Petro Dollar.Petro Yuan. Petro Rupee?" Gateway House Paper No 19, June 2019.
2 U.S. Department of Justice. 2015. "U.S. and Five Gulf States Reach Historic Settlement with BP to Resolve Civil Lawsuit Over Deepwater Horizon Oil Spill." https://www.justice.gov/opa/pr/us-and-five-gulf-states-reach-historic-settlement-bp-resolve-civil-lawsuit-over-deepwater
3 U.S. Department of Justice. 2017. "Volkswagen AG Agrees to Plead Guilty and Pay \$4.3 Billion in Criminal and Civil Penalties; Six Volkswagen Executives and Employees are Indicted in Connection with Conspiracy to Cheat U.S. Emissions Tests". https://www.justice.gov/opa/pr/volkswagen-ag-agrees-plead-guilty-and-pay-43-billion-criminal-and-civil-penalties-six
4 U.S. Department of Justice. 2014. "BNP Paribas Agrees to Plead Guilty and to Pay \$8.9 Billion for Illegally Processing Financial Transactions for Countries Subject to U.S. Economic Sanctions". https://www.justice.gov/opa/pr/bnp-paribas-agrees-plead-guilty-and-pay-89-billion-illegally-processing-financial
5 World Bank. n.d. "GDP (Current US\$) – China, United States, India | Data." *Data.worldbank.org.* Accessed April 6, 2021. https://data.worldbank.org/indicator/NY.GDP.MKTP.CD?locations=CN-US-IN&year_high_desc=true
6 PricewaterhouseCoopers. 2016. "The World in 2050: PwC." PwC. 2016. https://www.pwc.com/gx/en/issues/economy/the-world-in-2050.html
7 Recknagel, Charles. 2000. "Iraq: Baghdad Moves to Euro." Radio FreeEurope/RadioLiberty. 2000. https://www.rferl.org/a/1095057.html

8 Reuters. 2016. "China Lays out Its Vision to Become a Tech Power." *Reuters*, March 5, 2016. https://www.reuters.com/article/us-china-parliament-tech-idUSKCN0W707Z

9 Shanghai International Exchange Energy. "INF Futures Contracts Report." www.ine.cn. http://www.ine.cn/en/statements/daily/?paramid=kx

10 ICE Report Center - Data," The ICE.

11 CME Group, "Energy Futures Products."

12 Bloomberg. 2018. "Speculators Rattle China Oil Futures as Prices Break from World." *Bloomberg.com*, August 7, 2018. https://www.bloomberg.com/news/articles/2018-08-07/oil-speculators-grip-china-futures-as-prices-post-mystery-gains

13 Wong, Edward, Neil Gough, and Alexandra Stevenson. 2015. "China's Response to Stock Plunge Rattles Traders." *The New York Times*, September 9, 2015, sec. World. https://www.nytimes.com/2015/09/10/world/asia/in-china-a-forceful-crackdown-in-response-to-stock-market-crisis.html

14 Organization of the Petroleum Exporting Countries. 2017. "2017 OPEC World Oil Outlook." https://www.opec.org/opec_web/flipbook/WOO2017/WOO2017/assets/common/downloads/WOO%202017.pdf

15 Valencia, Fabian. "To Hedge or to Self-insure? The Benefits of Mexico's Oil Hedging Program." https://www.imf.org/external/np/blog/dialogo/032618.pdf

16 Blas, Javier, and Catherine Ngai. 2018. "Mexico Takes First Steps in Annual Oil Hedging Program." *Bloomberg.com*, May 11, 2018. https://www.bloomberg.com/news/articles/2018-05-11/mexico-is-said-to-take-first-steps-in-annual-oil-hedging-program

17 The World Bank. 2016. "Uruguay Partners with the World Bank to Reduce its Exposure to Oil Price Volatility." https://www.worldbank.org/en/news/press-release/2016/06/15/uruguay-se-asocia-con-banco-mundial-para-reducir-su-exposicion-a-volatilidad-del-precio-del-petroleo

18 Mcintosh, Douglas. 2015. "Jamaica Hedges 8 Million Barrels of Crude in Deal with Citibank." https://jis.gov.jm/jamaica-hedges-8-million-barrels-of-crude-in-deal-with-citibank/

19 Petroleum Planning & Analysis Cell. 2019. "Monthly Report on Indigenous Crude Oil Production, Import And Processing & Production, Import and Export of Petroleum Products." New Delhi: PPAC, Ministry of Petroleum and Natural Gas. https://ppac.gov.in/WriteReadData/Reports/201905130115553480123WebVersion_MonthlyReportMarch2019.pdf

20 Petroleum Planning & Analysis Cell. 2019. "PPAC's Snapshot of India's Oil and Gas Data." New Delhi: PPAC, Ministry of Petroleum and Natural Gas. https://www.ppac.gov.in/WriteReadData/Reports/201905020429288786567SnapshotofIndiasOilandGasData_March2019.pdf

21 Petroleum Planning & Analysis Cell. 2019. "Domestic Natural gas Price for the Period October, 2019 – March, 2020." https://www.ppac.gov.in/WriteReadData/CMS/201909300543402696331DomesticNaturalGasPricefortheperiodOctober2019toMarch2020.pdf

22 Ministry of Petroleum and Natural Gas, Government of India. "Oil Storage Bunkers." Lok Sabha. Question 3184. http://loksabhaph.nic.in/Questions/QResult15.aspx?qref=76602&lsno=16

23 Tuttle, Robert. 2018. "The Most-Hedged U.S. Airlines Are Paying Higher Fuel Prices." Bloomberg.com. Bloomberg. February 16, 2018. https:// www.bloomberg.com/news/articles/2018-02-16/the-most-hedged-u-s-airlines-are-paying-higher-fuel-prices
24 Quinn, Dale. 2019. "Mexico Confirms It Completed 2019 Oil Hedge at $55 a Barrel." *Bloomberg.com*, January 10, 2019. https://www.bloomberg.com/news/articles/2019-01-10/mexico-finance-ministry-completes-oil-hedges-at-55-a-barrel

5 Meeting India's energy challenge

India's energy challenge, simply put, is to be able to source its growing energy needs at an affordable price. To understand this problem better, we need to understand how India uses energy. The country's energy consumption can be understood as two big baskets – electricity and transport. Electricity is lower value and relies largely on coal, while transportation relies largely on oil. Every other fuel in India's energy mix is either a substitute for oil or a substitute for coal. Hydropower, nuclear power and renewable energy are substitutes for coal, while natural gas straddles both baskets – it can be used as a vehicle fuel (CNG) and is used to generate a small amount of electricity (too expensive for wider use).

Coal accounts for over half of all primary energy consumption in India. It accounts for almost 75% of all electricity generation and is also used in sectors such as steel. However, nearly 80% of India's coal requirements are met domestically, with the remainder being imported from Australia, South Africa and Indonesia. The availability of coal is not going to be an issue for India. It is also unlikely that coal will be meaningfully replaced by any of the three substitutes – hydro, nuclear and renewable energy. India's hydropower potential is concentrated in hilly regions, construction of dams is expensive and time-consuming and power generation is seasonal – much of it happens during and after the monsoon. Thus, hydropower is unlikely to grow much beyond its current share of the mix. Nuclear power is too expensive to be a viable option, project execution has been slow, and there are also widespread fears about radiation in the aftermath of Fukushima – meaning new projects will face delays due to protests. Renewable energy is intermittent and cannot be scaled up without viable solutions for power storage, which don't exist at this point. The electricity basket is unlikely to see a major transformation in the foreseeable future.

In the case of transport, almost all vehicles – two-wheelers, cars, trucks and even aircraft – require petroleum products. Natural gas,

DOI: 10.4324/9781003152927-5

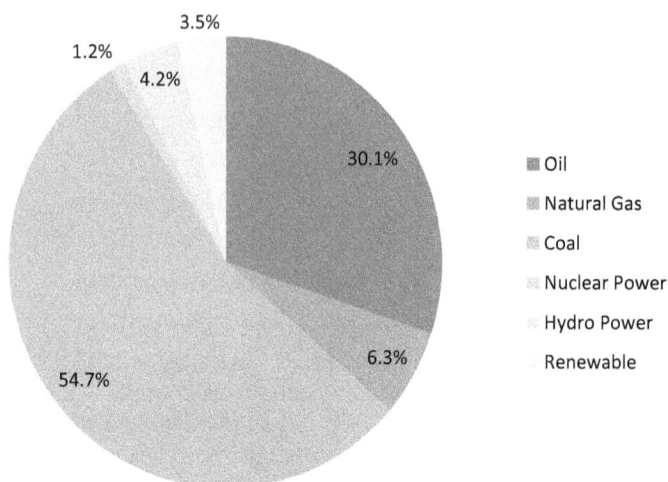

Figure 5.1 India's Energy Mix (2018)
Source: BP Statistical Review.

in the form of CNG, is an alternative in some urban areas—Delhi, Mumbai and parts of Gujarat at present. Natural gas is also an alternative to petroleum products as a cooking fuel [Piped Natural Gas (PNG) against LPG)] and an industrial fuel. However, any additional consumption of either fuel will have to be met via imports – India doesn't have enough oil or natural gas, which is unlikely to change. The impact of new technologies such as electric vehicles is likely to be very limited in the near future.

Considering these factors, India's energy dilemma boils down to one question – how to source the required quantity of oil and natural gas at an affordable price, minimising the impact of geopolitical disruptions on prices and supplies.

The previous chapters have drawn out how the energy world is changing, what India has done to secure oil supplies, key geopolitical choke points and the potential use of financial markets for securing energy. This chapter looks at specific recommendations to deal with those issues.

Recommendation 1: build new partnerships, invest in stable, oil-rich countries: the US, Canada

India's overseas oil investments have so far been done looking at the rear-view mirror – and have focussed on countries traditionally considered oil rich – Russia, Venezuela, Iran, etc. India needs to look at the two biggest stories in the oil patch – the US and Canada, which have between them added over 10 million barrels per day of fresh oil supply over the last decade. These countries are oil rich, politically and economically stable, are governed by rule of law and protect the rights of foreign investors. All this comes at a price, and historically, acquiring energy assets in the US or Canada was an expensive proposition. But the current low price of oil makes investments in these countries financially viable. The share prices of US oil independents such as Occidental, Marathon and Devon – each a large company in its own right, are at a fraction of the levels 10 or even five years back.

India will face a problem here – most of India's oil and gas companies are owned by the government, and outright acquisition of the US or Canadian oil company by an Indian state-owned enterprise is no longer possible in either country. China's CNOOC first tried to acquire US oil firm Unocal in 2005 and then successfully acquired Canada's oil sand producer Nexen in 2012. The first acquisition was disallowed while the Canadian government made it clear that the second acquisition will be the last of its kind. Both the countries now have laws dealing with such situations.[1]

While India is not a geopolitical threat or a rival like China, a proposed acquisition by a state-owned enterprise may run into opposition. Second, the assets in the US and Canada are unique – oil shale and oil sands – which require unique local know-how, which Indian oil companies do not have. India's top oil producer, ONGC, primarily produces from conventional fields, while others – IOC and BPCL, are primarily refining and marketing companies with even less expertise in oil production. Finally, stringent environmental norms in the US and Canada also mean that there can be multibillion-dollar penalties in case of an accident or a violation. This is a headache the public sector oil companies can do well without.

Therefore, the ideal approach should be to acquire minority stakes in these companies, purely as a financial investor. For an oil company, a minority stake without management control may not be worthwhile – because you can no longer show reserves of the acquired asset as a part of your reserves. Also, the mandate of an operating company is to invest in business, not in someone else's business. Such investment will be better made by a purpose-created Sovereign Wealth Fund (SWF), which can invest in a basket of US and Canadian energy companies. SWFs from across the world invest in the US financial markets without restrictions – and an Indian SWF shouldn't face a problem either.

Recommendation 2: deepen existing partnerships with Saudi Arabia, the UAE and Kuwait

As discussed in Chapter 3, India's oil and gas imports from the Persian Gulf pass close to the Pakistani port of Gwadar. Moreover, a large part of India's energy infrastructure is concentrated in the Gulf of Kutch, close to Pakistan. Both of these are vulnerable to hostile action by Pakistan, which has in the past shown itself as a malign player. India's direct leverage on Pakistan, to dissuade it from such behaviour, is non-existent. However, India can create an indirect leverage on Pakistan, via its economic relations with the oil-rich Gulf countries – Saudi Arabia, the UAE and Kuwait.

Pakistan has major financial dependence on all three. Millions of Pakistanis work in the Gulf monarchies, and their remittances are a major part of Pakistan's forex earnings. During FY20, Pakistan received total inward remittance of $23 billion, of which over half came from the GCC, and just two countries – Saudi Arabia and the UAE, accounted for over $10 billion. For a country facing a perennial balance of payments crisis, these are big numbers. Saudi Arabia and the UAE have also extended loans to Pakistan during its recent economic crisis,[2] while Saudi Arabia also agreed to provide oil to Pakistan on deferred payment.[3]

While Pakistan's relations with the Gulf monarchies are those of a client state, India's relations are much more equal. India's relations with these three states have undergone a change in recent years, as it has become a major oil importer, and important for the prosperity of oil exporters. This importance can be seen in the way India–UAE and India–Saudi Arabia ties have shifted. In 2019, India was invited to participate in the meeting of the Organization of Islamic Countries (OIC), as a 'guest of honour', evidently a result of Prime Minister Modi's outreach to Saudi Arabia and the UAE.[4] Pakistan, a founding member of the OIC, boycotted the meeting in protest.[5] Saudi Arabia and the UAE have both expressed their interest in a deeper partnership with India by taking up stakes in India's downstream petroleum refining and fuel retail business. The UAE has also licensed ONGC to explore for oil from one of its offshore blocks.

Bringing in Saudi Arabia and the UAE as investors in India's growing downstream oil & gas industry will ensure that any hostile action by Pakistan will directly impact its two major benefactors. Reliance, by proposing to bring in Saudi Aramco as an investor, has shown the way. The same approach could be followed for the public sector energy majors – Indian Oil and Bharat Petroleum. India should encourage the sovereign wealth funds of the Gulf monarchies to invest in downstream oil infrastructure here.

Recommendation 3: increase the use of natural gas

Natural gas is the closest substitute for oil. In the form of CNG, it can be used as a vehicle fuel and can replace diesel and petrol. In the form of PNG, it is a replacement for LPG (cooking gas). Compared to oil, natural gas has a different geographical distribution. Earlier, the export of natural gas was restricted to countries that could be reached via a pipeline – this is no longer the case as the liquefied natural gas trade has expanded.

India can import natural gas only via the LNG route – which also means it can import gas anywhere from the world. Large-scale production of shale gas in the US and construction of LNG terminals in Australia means that there are two new players in this market – not vulnerable to the geopolitics and unrest of West Asia. Russia, which is the world's largest gas producer, is also trying to diversify its customer base by building LNG terminals on its northern coast. This will enable Russia to tap into the wider global market, rather than being restricted to Europe and China.

Increasing the use of natural gas will automatically result in reduced dependence on oil and will help diversify India's energy imports away from geopolitically volatile states. Also, increasing imports from the US and Australia will also help as India tries to build a closer partnership with the US and Australia in the Indo-Pacific (the Quad).

Recommendation 4: use financial markets for energy security

As detailed in Chapter 4, India needs to use its inherent advantages – transparent and rule-driven financial markets – to secure its energy needs. From being a price taker in the global energy markets, India needs to become a price-maker. The detailed arguments about how facilitating this trade can help improve India's energy security have already been spelled out in Chapter 4.

Specifically, India should encourage mutual fund houses to launch an Exchange Traded Fund (ETF) for crude oil – just as there are multiple ETFs for gold. This ETF can be sold to investors and will serve as a de-facto Strategic Petroleum Reserve (SPR) during an emergency – reducing the burden on the public exchequer. Second, the physical settlement should be permitted in the crude oil trade that happens on Indian exchanges – and ETFs should be allowed as acceptable units for this settlement. This will automatically create a large group of sellers in futures/options in the case of oil. This will help overcome India's inherent disadvantage – a lack of oil producers/sellers. In the longer run, India needs to encourage foreign participation. Just as India's stock market permits the participation of foreign investors, the commodity markets must also be open to foreign oil sellers.

Historically, per-1947, India was the economic centre of the Indian Ocean rim and the Indian rupee was the default currency of the region. As India's economy regains the lost ground, India must restore the old economic linkages and ties with other economies of the region. This will enable India to not only ensure a better deal for its citizens working in the Gulf countries (over 8 million) but will also allow it to counter China's growing influence and will create a point of leverage over Pakistan – making India's energy infrastructure and energy flows more secure.

Recommendation 5: focus on outcomes, not technologies

In 2019, Niti Aayog, India's planning department, suggested in media statements that it was time to go all electric and that after 2030, only electric vehicles would be sold in India.[6] This was projected as a magic bullet that would solve India's problems of very high levels of urban pollution and also cut down the large oil import bill.

This is unlikely to happen for a host of reasons. First, the constraints in the EV supply chain – lithium, rare earths and cobalt, and the problems in scaling these supply chains up by 25–50×. Second, China's near complete monopoly on supply of rare earths. Third, the technology doesn't work outside a narrow sphere (cars) – for instance, electric trucks will need to carry half their total weight in batteries if they are to match diesel trucks.

Governments across the world have proven notoriously bad at picking winners – and it is not the government's job to pick winners either. Selecting one unproven technology as the answer to all our problems is not a sound approach. If the government wants cleaner air, it can mandate emission norms for vehicles – which companies can now meet through whatever works, rather than mandating that only one technology will be used. If the objective is to improve India's energy security, it is not clear how replacing a supply chain that has worked well for 70 years with a new, unproven supply chain with multiple bottlenecks will do that.

Enthusiasts and evangelists get carried away with magic bullet technologies – governments cannot afford to do that.

Recommendation 6: avoid the same mistakes, again

Every few years, policymakers in India and elsewhere flirt with biofuels. Sometimes it is because the price of conventional oil is too high, at other times, it is because we want to reduce our carbon footprint. Biofuels have been proven to be a bad, unworkable idea repeatedly, in different spheres. It almost seems as if biofuels are the answer waiting for a problem. At present, it is being pitched as an idea to reduce dependence on imported oil (which it won't), but the unstated and real benefit may be that it provides income support for sugarcane farmers (which may be more justified).

Unfortunately, sugarcane is one of the thirstier crops that are cultivated in India. Agricultural land and water are both finite resources – if they are used to cultivate fuel, it will reduce the land available for food cultivation and push up food prices. In 2008, the global fascination for biofuels also resulted in the highest ever food price inflation, in a generation. As India increasingly grapples with shortages of cultivable land and potable water, experiments with such a large disruptive potential are best avoided. Policymakers need to avoid solutions that cause new, bigger problems compared to what they solve.

Notes

1 https://www.gatewayhouse.in/petro-state/
2 https://www.bloomberg.com/news/articles/2019-01-25/saudi-u-a-e-loans-to-help-pakistan-avert-financial-crisis
3 https://www.arabnews.com/node/1519401/pakistan
4 https://www.livemint.com/politics/news/india-invited-as-guest-of-honour-to-oic-meet-sushma-swaraj-to-attend-1550913750935.html
5 https://www.khaleejtimes.com/international/india-pakistan-standoff/pakistani-minister-boycotts-oic-meeting-in-abu-dhabi-over-indian-presence
6 https://timesofindia.indiatimes.com/india/nitis-new-road-map-only-electric-vehicles-to-be-sold-after-2030/articleshow/69833770.cms

Index

Note: **Bold** page numbers refer to tables; *italic* page numbers refer to figures.

For Product Safety Concerns and Information please contact our EU
representative GPSR@taylorandfrancis.com
Taylor & Francis Verlag GmbH, Kaufingerstraße 24, 80331 München, Germany